*Old Testament
Stories from the
Back Side*

Old Testament Stories from the Back Side

J. ELLSWORTH KALAS

Abingdon Press
NASHVILLE

OLD TESTAMENT STORIES FROM THE BACK SIDE

Copyright © 1995 by Abingdon Press

This book is printed on acid-free, recycled paper.

Library of Congress Cataloging-in-Publication Data

Kalas, J. Ellsworth, 1923–
    Old Testament stories from the back side/J. Ellsworth Kalas.
        p.   cm.
    ISBN 0-687-08186-6 (alk. paper)
    1. Bible stories, English—O.T.   I. Title.
BS1140.2.K34   1995
221.6—dc20   95-12000
                                                                      CIP

Except for brief paraphrases or unless otherwise noted, scripture quotations are from the New Revised Standard Version Bible, copyright 1989 by the Division of Christian Education of the National Council of the Churches of Christ in the U.S.A. Used by permission.

Those noted NIV are from the HOLY BIBLE, NEW INTERNATIONAL VERSION® Copyright © 1973, 1978, 1984 by International Bible Society. Used by permission of Zondervan Publishing House. All rights reserved.

Those noted GNB are from the *Good News Bible*—Old Testament: Copyright © American Bible Society 1976; New Testament: Copyright © American Bible Society 1966, 1971, 1976.

99 00 01 02 03 04—10 9 8

MANUFACTURED IN THE UNITED STATES OF AMERICA

To Janet

CONTENTS

Contents

INTRODUCTION

I have loved the Old Testament and its stories longer than I can remember. Somewhere in the photographs of my memory is a book my mother read to me, from a day and a world when there were not many books and when pictures and typography were not naturally attractive; yet this book captured me, and we came back to it again and again—a child's book of Bible stories, most of them from the Old Testament.

There were also Sunday school teachers, and weekly picture cards, fully half of them portraying Old Testament stories.

And then, the Bible itself. I first read it through as an eleven-year-old, and even though the majestic language of the King James Version may at times have been hard to understand, I found the stories wonderfully alive. They became part of the fabric of my commitment to God, and were my instructors in a path of discipleship. The characters became my friends. Some, like David, I embraced; Saul made me sad, and Gideon made me smile. As I entered a world of literature, I realized that Jephthah was more tragic than Willie Loman, and that Hamlet could have learned his indecision from Balaam. And of course David and Bathsheba prepared the way for Hester Prynne and the Reverend Dimmesdale. I came to feel that no textbook in psychology could be more revealing of our human condition than are these stories of women and men who struggled with themselves, with one another, and with God. Each time I read their stories, I understand myself and life a little better, and I love God more.

I'm approaching these stories from the back side—that is, from an unconventional or perhaps an unlikely route. Perhaps this approach reflects my lifetime of reading the Bible, or an even longer lifetime of listening to (and later, preaching) sermons. Or perhaps it's simply a reflection of my own personality. At any rate, I enjoy coming at these wonderful people and experiences in ways that help me to see them in new light—and thus to teach me new lessons.

I hope that you will have the same experience as you enter these stories with me. In the process, I hope you'll be inspired to read your Bible with new excitement. And if by chance you also decide to read some of these chapters a second time, I'll be glad. God bless!

J. Ellsworth Kalas

*Old Testament
Stories from the
Back Side*

The Second Sin

GENESIS 3:1-13: Now the serpent was more crafty than any other wild animal that the LORD God had made. He said to the woman, "Did God say, 'You shall not eat from any tree in the garden'?" The woman said to the serpent, "We may eat of the fruit of the trees in the garden; but God said, 'You shall not eat of the fruit of the tree that is in the middle of the garden, nor shall you touch it, or you shall die.' " But the serpent said to the woman, "You will not die; for God knows that when you eat of it your eyes will be opened, and you will be like God, knowing good and evil." So when the woman saw that the tree was good for food, and that it was a delight to the eyes, and that the tree was to be desired to make one wise, she took of its fruit and ate; and she also gave some to her husband, who was with her, and he ate. Then the eyes of both were opened, and they knew that they were naked; and they sewed fig leaves together and made loincloths for themselves.

They heard the sound of the LORD God walking in the garden at the time of the evening breeze, and the man and his wife hid themselves from the presence of the LORD God among the trees of the garden. But the LORD God called to the man, and said to him, "Where are you?" He said, "I heard the sound of you in the garden, and I was afraid, because I was naked; and I hid myself." He said, "Who told you that you were naked? Have you eaten from the tree of which I commanded you not to eat?" The man said, "The woman whom you gave to be with me, she gave me fruit from the tree, and I ate." Then the LORD God said to the woman, "What is this that you have done?" The woman said, "The serpent tricked me, and I ate."

I keep worrying about the second sin. Philosophers wonder about the first sin, and the average person doesn't usually keep count; but I worry about the second sin.

Part of my worry comes from the feeling that I'm the only one concerned about the second sin. And of course it is so subtle. That's why so few are thinking about it, which naturally makes my burden all the greater.

But before we go farther, let's review the circumstances of the first sin, since this is where the whole issue begins. You remember the story. Adam and Eve were living in an utterly perfect setting, in a place so ideal that they called it Eden—*paradise.* It seemed they had everything their hearts could desire. The only thing forbidden to them was the fruit of the tree of the knowledge of good and evil.

One day a spectacular visitor, the serpent, struck up a conversation with Eve. We don't know why he ignored Adam, who was with her (Genesis 3:6), and spoke to her, nor why she carried the whole weight of the conversation. The serpent raised in Eve's mind a question about the goodness of God: Why would God refuse her and Adam the privilege of anything in the Garden, especially something that obviously must be the most desirable thing there? And then, an accusation: God refuses you this particular fruit because God knows you will become equal to the Divine if you eat it.

So Eve was convinced, and she ate. And being generous by nature, she shared the fruit with her husband, and he ate. And that was the first sin.

Of course that story doesn't satisfy us; it only quickens our curiosity. What, exactly, was that first sin? Some have suggested that it was the discovery of sex, because Adam and Eve became conscious of their nakedness and made themselves garments of fig leaves. But that explanation misses the point, even if it succeeds in making the story more exciting. The issue was the human desire to be equal with God.

The Bible, in its profound wisdom, portrays the first sin in entirely symbolic language. If it had described the sin as the violation of a specific commandment, we humans would ever after have thought that act to be the worst sin and probably the only one to worry about; and I expect we then would have been unconcerned about all the others. But the writer of Genesis simply gives us a picture: The first sin is the eating of the forbidden fruit. It is the basic act of disobedience and disbelief. As such it is the essence of our human problem.

This first sin is highly significant because it's the first. But the second sin may, in fact, be more important—because we'll never recover from the first sin so long as we're guilty of the second. The scriptures and human experience both testify that God has provided a remedy for the first sin, no matter what it is. But the second sin can make God's remedy ineffective. That's why it worries me so. One might even say that the second sin is the unpardonable sin. And yet, you don't hear anything about the second sin, do you?

Let's go back to the Bible story to see how it all happened. After Adam and Eve had eaten the forbidden fruit, they became ashamed of their nakedness; but far more important, they became uneasy about God. So when God came walking in the Garden soon thereafter, Adam and Eve tried to hide. They must have realized that it is impossible to hide from God, but sin makes us humans do irrational things; sin is never very smart, you know, not even when it dresses itself in sophistication. "Why are you hiding?" God asked. And Adam, who had been quite silent in the conversations with the serpent, replied, "I heard you coming and didn't want you to see me naked. So I hid."

Now God pressed the matter. "Who told you that you were naked? Have you eaten fruit from the tree about which I warned you?"

Adam answered, "Yes, but it was the woman you gave me who brought me some, and I ate it." And Eve, not to be left bearing sole responsibility, chimed in, "The serpent tricked me."

Now there you have the second sin. It is even more dangerous than the first, because it prevents our recovering from the first. It is the sin of *excuses*—the unwillingness to admit that we are wrong and the refusal to see ourselves for what we are. Whatever our original sin may be, whether it is lying, adultery, cheating, ill temper, gluttony, drunkenness, gossip, or murder, there is always hope for us. But when we become guilty of the second sin, the sin of excusing ourselves and of being unwilling to face ourselves, we close the door against God and hope.

Eliezer ben Hyrcanus, a second-century rabbi, said, "Like an architect, the Holy One modeled the world, and it would not stand, until He created repentance." The world does, indeed, stand or fall with our readiness to repent. This is true of nations, of institutions, of individuals. If a nation takes a wrong road and repents, she can recover; but if she insists on justifying her policies, she will disintegrate. It may be a slow process, but it is a sure one. The prophets called it the judgment of God, but it is written into the very nature of the universe. Either we face ourselves and repent, or our world falls.

The same rule applies to institutions. When investigative reporters revealed that a national charitable organization was paying exorbitant salaries to a few top officers and that money was being used recklessly, the organization could either tough it out or admit it had erred. It chose to confess its sins, and it survived. I doubt that the public would have continued its support if that organization had done anything less than make an abject apology to the nation. But the key word is not "abject"; it is repentance.

Fiorello La Guardia, whose name has been taken by both an airport and a musical, was the flamboyant but effective mayor of New York City from 1934 to 1945. He was an institution! But he made mistakes and acknowledged them. He noted that he didn't make many and said, "But when I do, it's a beaut!" His voters laughed with him, because he knew enough to acknowledge when he was wrong.

Mistakes don't destroy us, nor will the eternal mistakes called sins; what destroys is our inability to face ourselves and confess that we've been wrong. If a ballplayer can't catch the ball, there's still hope if he will say to his coach, "I must be doing something wrong." But there's almost no hope for the person who insists on excusing his errors: the sun got in my eyes; the grass was wet; I thought Jim was going to catch it. So it is in the world of learning. Those who make the most of the educational enterprise are not necessarily those with a high I.Q. The secret is to be teachable; and to be teachable you must be willing to admit that you don't know—and that's a form of repentance: repenting of ignorance. As long as we excuse our failure to learn, we frustrate the learning process.

But baseball and even learning are relatively inconsequential compared with the issues of the soul, our very being. The personalities of the Bible might easily be divided into those who were willing to learn—that is, to repent—and those who were not. Those two categories could also be classified as the victorious and the tragic. Moses and Balaam both erred, but Moses repented his way to greatness while Balaam died a fool. Saul and David were both sinners, dramatically flawed, but Saul exited in tragedy while David was declared a person after God's own heart.

Some of history's most magnificent human beings have been marked by major sins, mistakes, and befuddlements, yet they have come to greatness because of their capacity for acknowledging their failures. They are great, in some instances, not in spite of their sins but because of them. Character grows out of the soil of our lives like a tender plant. If we repent of our sins, repentance breaks the soil of life so that the plant gets a new and stronger start. But if we excuse or ignore our failures, the soil of life hardens until the plant of character simply cannot survive.

I have suggested that the second sin may be what is often called "the unpardonable sin." The unpardonable sin is defined as the sin against the Holy Spirit (Mark 3:28, 29), a blaspheming of the

Spirit of God. The Holy Spirit is the persuasive agent in our lives, the power which convicts us of sin. When we excuse ourselves and refuse to recognize our sins, we harden ourselves against the Spirit's work of persuasion. That very act of resisting and hardening is a sin against the Spirit—a blaspheming, so to speak, of the Spirit's work. If this rejection continues long enough, we come to a place where we no longer hear or sense the Spirit's pleading. How could we be more lost than to be in a state where we are no longer disturbed about being wrong? We come to such a place by the continuing process of self-excusing.

What experts we are in hiding from the knowledge of what we are! Adam and Eve set the pattern for us, and we've been refining it ever since. When God asked Adam if he had eaten from the forbidden tree, he had the opportunity to step forward and confess what he had done. Instead he answered, "Yes, but the woman . . ." What a courageous soul he was: brave, ready to shoulder responsibility! "It was the woman."

And the woman, I regret to say, did no better. Several differences exist between the sexes, but sin isn't one of them. Male and female, we have a common facility for excusing ourselves. While it is often noted that the woman committed the first sin, it must also be said that the man led the way on the second. And in both cases, the other was all too prompt to follow. So when Eve saw the blame heading toward her, she quickly said, "The serpent tricked me." One remembers comedian Flip Wilson whose character Geraldine would excuse all her failures with, "The devil made me do it." When we see Geraldine, we have a sad-funny caricature of us all.

But I'm not done with Adam. His excuse doesn't stop with shifting the burden of blame to Eve. He complains to God, "It was *the woman you gave me.*" In other words, "It's your fault, God, for so generously providing me with this lovely creature who leads me astray—this one of whom I said so recently that she was bone of my bone and flesh of my flesh. It's your fault for giving her to me."

We've been talking to God that way ever since. "It's the temperament you gave me. I can't help myself." "It's in my genes." "It's my lack of talent. If only God had given me more talent." An American actress once explained the tragedies of her troubled life by her beauty: She had become beautiful when she was too young to handle such a responsibility. Others blame the stars. And such a response is nothing new; Shakespeare had his Cassius correct Brutus:

> The fault, dear Brutus, is not in our stars,
> But in ourselves . . .
>
> (*JULIUS CAESAR*, I, ii)

Even so, perhaps we have refined the skills of earlier generations. Our great learning has given us new ways to excuse ourselves. Vast numbers use psychiatry and its related sciences to aid and abet their natural inclination to blame someone else. Jerome Ellison, a premier magazine editor from the middle years of this century, recalls that he spent many thousands of dollars with several psychiatrists to cure himself of alcoholism, and the whole experience ended with the feeling that his parents had failed him in his infancy. Later Ellison wisely concluded that it did no good to blame his parents for the state he was in. That wasn't really the issue. Now the only point was to see what he could do with the life he had and the mess he had made of it. For all of us, that means stripping ourselves of all excuses and making a new start.

Our knowledge is leading us, it seems, to a veritable epidemic of fault-displacement. George A. Tobin, the Washington attorney and writer, recalls an acquaintance who excused his various moral lapses by saying, "Well, I'm just the kinda guy who. . ." All of us have known such a person; some of us have sometimes been such a person! But now we have science, of sorts, on our side. We're quite sure we can find secrets in our genetic code to prove that we're really not responsible for what we do. "What can one expect of a person whose intricate makeup is like mine?" we ask. There's something both perverse and amusing about the fact that some who scorn the idea of a devil have shaped a devil of their own and have christened it in the name of science.

The ultimate tragedy of the second sin is that it prevents us from finding God. The ancient poet cried out in his guilt:

> The sacrifice acceptable to God is a broken spirit;
> a broken and contrite heart, O God, you will not despise.
>
> (PSALM 51:17)

God can visit the penitent soul because the penitent soul has an open door. But God is shut out of the life that covers over its failures with a hard surface of excuses. The Forgiving One never has opportunity to forgive and restore those who will not acknowledge that they want such a divine Friend.

When Adam and Eve sinned, a great mercy came into their lives. God called, "Where are you?" When you're trying to run from yourself and from God and from life, that call doesn't at first seem a mercy. In his epic poem "The Hound of Heaven," Francis Thompson describes God as one whom we flee "down the vistas of the years." But kindly and persistently, God pursues us, hounds us, follows after us.

I imagine a community that has been devastated by a fatal epidemic. Now a physician comes who has a sure, accessible remedy. Through the streets of the village he walks, past closed doors, crying out as in ancient Eden, "Where are you? Where are you?"

Some hide in the basements of life and die. But others sense the mercy in the cry and recognize that as painful as it may be to confess the possibility of their infection, they must submit themselves to treatment so that their lives can be saved.

Shall we say to the physician, "My neighbor is responsible . . . the woman you gave me." "I was born with a constitutional weakness, and the environment is against me." "The system is bad. Who can get well with a system like the one where I live?" No, no! Say, "I'm infected. Please heal me. *Please make me well.*"

Whatever sin or weakness or inadequacy affects and afflicts us, God offers the remedy. Only one thing can prevent our getting well. Only *one!* The second sin. Our innate unwillingness to confess that we need help—and on the basis of that confession, to seek God's remedy.

Whatever we do with this life, whatever course we follow, let us be sure that we don't die making excuses.

CHAPTER 2

The Importance of
Naming Joseph

GENESIS 30:22-24: Then God remembered Rachel, and God heeded her and opened her womb. She conceived and bore a son, and said, "God has taken away my reproach"; and she named him Joseph, saying, "May the LORD add to me another son!"

*H*er name was Rachel, and if in her day there had been a magazine such as *Town and Country* or *People*, she would have been featured in its pages. They would have said that she had it made. She was beautiful, she was the daughter of a wealthy man, and her husband, Jacob, was a rising young entrepreneur—the kind of man you knew would someday be fabulously rich. And above all, she was loved—so much loved, in fact, that her husband agreed to work fourteen years to have her as his wife. She did, for sure, have everything going for her.

But one thing was missing, and to her it was such a big thing that it took the bloom off all those other things that made others envy her. She wasn't able to have a child.

We can understand her pain. After all, one of the most significant and growing areas of modern medicine specializes in helping couples conceive. But in Rachel's culture, the issue was more than just the innate human desire to become a parent. In her world, children were looked upon not only as a blessing from God, but also as primary evidence of God's favor. Those who didn't have children were perceived as suffering from God's disapproval. And unfair though it was, it also was assumed that it must be the woman with whom God was displeased, not her husband.

In Rachel's case, the rudimentary evidence was against her. Her older sister also was married to Jacob, and she had no trouble at all in conceiving and bearing children. Without a doubt some sisterly rivalry added to the pain. Everyone knew that Jacob had married the older sister, Leah, under duress and that it was Rachel he wanted; so of course Leah felt some justification in her ability to have children. Perhaps she even let Rachel know that while Jacob might prefer her, God was smiling on Leah. Even more disconcerting to Rachel was the realization that Jacob's line, name, and inheritance would be carried through Leah. The line and name of Rachel would gradually be lost.

So Rachel fretted and fumed and chided Jacob, until Jacob became angry. "Am I God," he said, "that I can decide whether or not you will have a child?" But eventually, the writer of Genesis tells us, "God remembered Rachel" (how good is the memory of God, even if not always as quick as we might wish), and God "opened her womb" (Genesis 30:22).

So her prayer was answered, the prayer she had spoken so long, with so much anguish and earnestness. Rachel not only had a child; she had a son—and in her time and culture, that was very special because the family line and wealth ordinarily passed through the male members of the family. We don't know for sure how long Rachel waited for this child, but we can reasonably calculate that it was at least ten years, perhaps longer.

"So what shall we name this child, this answer to prayer, this gift of God, this tiny and wonderful miracle?" Rachel must have said.

You see, in Old Testament times people didn't choose names casually. It wasn't a matter of what was currently in vogue. After more than four decades of baptizing infants, I can often determine a person's age by his or her name, because in our culture names have a run of popularity, like television shows. But not so in the ancient world. People named children according to the spiritual convictions they held, or something significant about the time of birth. Our Puritan forebears lived by the same conviction; that's why there were so many children with names such as Hope, Perseverance, Fortitude, and Increase.

So what name shall Rachel give to this miracle child? I can think of several appropriate names, and I'm sure you can, too. Probably you and I both sense that the name should carry a quality of gratitude, so it will convey the thanks and the wonder Rachel feels now that her longtime prayer has been answered.

Well, she named the baby Joseph, which means *May he* (God) *add*. Why did she name the boy "May God add"? Because, she said, "May the Lord add to me another son!"

Now how does that strike you? She had asked and asked and asked for a son, and now her request was granted. So did she say (profusely and endlessly and exuberantly) "Thank you"? No. She said, "Please send me another—same size, same model." And I have a feeling that there was a tone in her voice which added, "And hurry, please, because I'm not getting any younger."

Doesn't that seem more than a little ungrateful? Shouldn't Rachel have paused long enough to savor the flavor of her blessing before submitting another request? She reminds me of a four-year-old who, after taking one bite of his favorite food, promptly asks his mother for another helping. We discourage that attitude in preschoolers, and it seems unthinkable for an adult.

It wouldn't have been so bad if Rachel had chosen Joseph (may God add) for a middle name, and had used for a first name something like Chanan, which would have meant roughly, "God has shown me favor." Thus the boy's name would have been, so to speak, "Thanks for the favor; may I have another?" At least then she would have said *Thank you* before asking for something more.

And yet, as I look at the teachings of scripture, I have to say a word of praise for Rachel's choice of names. As a matter of fact, Rachel may have been a better theologian than we are. That is, she may have understood the nature of God more clearly and had a better understanding of the purposes of God in our lives.

Let me tell you how Rachel's prayer turned out. Rachel did indeed conceive again; we don't know how soon, because the Bible doesn't give any specifics about the time that elapsed. Unfortunately, Rachel had a difficult delivery with this second child, so difficult that the midwife felt she might not survive. As the child was born, the midwife encouraged Rachel: "Do not be afraid; for now you will have another son" (Genesis 35:17). That is, what Rachel had asked for in the naming of Joseph was now coming to pass. Rachel named this second son Benoni, which means "Son of my sorrow." And she died. But her husband, Jacob, changed the name, mercifully, to *Benjamin,* which means "Son of my right hand."

You may reason that if Rachel hadn't insisted on having another son, she wouldn't have lost her life in childbearing. But there's more to be said. Over the centuries Benjamin came to have a very special role. For one, his descendants were such courageous warriors that when the nation would go to battle the cry was, "After you, O Benjamin!" He was the only son of Jacob who was born in the "land of promise"—that is, the land that would eventually be known as the unique possession of the Jewish people. Although Benjamin was a small tribe, the first king of Israel, Saul, came from this body; and many generations later, the man known as Saul of Tarsus—the apostle Paul—also came from Benjamin's line. And when the time came that the nation of Israel divided, with the ten northern tribes separating themselves and eventually disappearing, the people of Benjamin chose to stay with those of Judah. Thus it can be said that probably half or nearly half of the people whom we know today as the Jewish people are descendants of Benjamin. Benjamin was indeed a key person in the history of the Jewish people, a kind of aristocracy of quality.

I'm impressed that Rachel knew there ought to be more to life than the blessing that came with her first son, the original answer to her prayer. We human beings are constantly afflicted with a kind of terminitis. We're always inclined to stop too soon. That's the problem, for example, with a high school or college diploma. It is an end worked toward, proudly achieved, and then made into a stopping place. In truth, it ought to be named *Joseph:* "May I add to it." Some of our ancestors rightly named the diploma-giving event "Commencement," to help us see that it is more of a beginning than an end, but we generally have a hard time living up to the "commencement" philosophy.

That's the way it is, too, with our faith-commitments. During my pastoral ministry I trained nearly forty confirmation classes and saw them through the sacred, beautiful Sunday of celebration. But I confess a sorrow about those classes: In too many cases, my students saw Confirmation Sunday as an end. Despite all that I said about confirmation as a starting point for the Christian life, some of my students saw it as a finish; they stopped attending Sunday school and gave little thought to joining the youth group. I wish I had named that Sunday *Joseph.*

The same sad admission must be made for many who experience a memorable conversion. We often call such an experience being "born again." That phrase surely suggests that it is only a beginning; after all, the purpose of birth is to produce, eventually, a full-grown person. But far too many see it as an end. Having been born again, they settle in to continuing spiritual infancy. When someone is born again, the day should be named *Joseph,* with the thematic question, "How can I get more?"

Rachel realized that God wasn't done with her yet. The fact that she had received one blessing—and a very big one, at that—did not mean that there was nothing more to be done or experienced. Instead, she saw it as the very opposite: Now that it was clear that she could have a baby, why not have two? If God had indicated that he wanted her to have a child, might he not also be pleased for her to have another?

I'm quite sure that our adversary would like for you and me to think that God's blessings have been exhausted in the kindness we have just received or the prayer that has just been answered. In truth, God's purpose is to make blessing number one a basis and a foundation for blessing number two—which, thanks be to God, will be greater than the original blessing because it builds upon it.

I think Rachel understood this. She realized that God had more in mind for this nomadic homemaker than that she would bear one son. Actually, she couldn't remotely have imagined just how great the purposes of God would ultimately be. I'm sure she couldn't have dreamed that a second son would father a people that would be significant in world history. Nor could she have imagined that someday, several thousand years later, a journeyman writer would tell her story to people in a part of the world she didn't know existed. No, she couldn't have imagined anything so vast and wonderful. But she did realize that God wasn't done with her yet, and that one son wasn't to be the end of her story—not if she had anything to say about it. And she did!

I'm sure that you and I often frustrate the purposes of God in our lives and in our churches because we think small and expect little. We sometimes call it humility or a lack of self-confidence. But whatever we name it, we're putting limits on the plan and purpose of God. And more than that, we are discrediting the generosity of God.

I am old enough to look back on my life and ponder the course it has taken. I testify gladly that I have received—as I perceive it—far more than my share of blessings. I've been privileged to do the work I love most and to enjoy a measure of achievement I couldn't have envisioned as a Depression-era boy. Yet I wonder: How much have I frustrated the purposes of God by my small expectations, or by my self-doubts? God has clearly thought better of me than I've thought of myself. Why have I been content to be only a halfway good human being, when I might have achieved so much more character, quality, and spiritual maturity?

I honor Rachel, most of all, because she believed in the goodness of God. She dared to ask largely of God because she believed that God is good, and that it would please God to bless her abundantly. C. S. Lewis once said that we are like ignorant children who want to go on making mud pies in a slum because they can't imagine what is meant by the offer of a holiday at the seaside. We're far too easily pleased. God wants us to expect more, to aim higher.

Hymnwriter Charles Wesley put it best of all when he asked himself how he could rightly thank God for the extraordinary blessings that had come his way:

> What shall I render to my God
> For all His mercy's store?
> I'll take the gifts He hath bestowed,
> And humbly ask for more.

Wesley had learned Rachel's secret: When you've prayed, waited, and worked to get something, and at last it comes, how can you thank God best? By accepting the divine kindness and recognizing that such goodness is the very essence of God's character—and then saying, "I'd like more of the same."

A remarkable woman, Rachel. Far more remarkable than any popular magazine article would have painted her. She wanted a son, wanted one desperately. So when the son came, she said, "I'll call him Joseph: *May God add.*" Give me still more! She understood the purpose and the goodness of God, and by doing so, she opened the door for God's goodness and purpose to be fulfilled. I wish I were more like her.

CHAPTER 3

Because
My Mother Told Me

EXODUS 2:1-10: Now a man from the house of Levi went and married a Levite woman. The woman conceived and bore a son; and when she saw that he was a fine baby, she hid him three months. When she could hide him no longer she got a papyrus basket for him, and plastered it with bitumen and pitch; she put the child in it and placed it among the reeds on the bank of the river. His sister stood at a distance, to see what would happen to him.

The daughter of Pharaoh came down to bathe at the river, while her attendants walked beside the river. She saw the basket among the reeds and sent her maid to bring it. When she opened it, she saw the child. He was crying, and she took pity on him, "This must be one of the Hebrews' children," she said. Then his sister said to Pharaoh's daughter, "Shall I go and get you a nurse from the Hebrew women to nurse the child for you?" Pharaoh's daughter said to her, "Yes." So the girl went and called the child's mother. Pharaoh's daughter said to her, "Take this child and nurse it for me, and I will give you your wages." So the woman took the child and nursed it. When the child grew up, she brought him to Pharaoh's daughter, and she took him as her son. She named him Moses, "because," she said, "I drew him out of the water."

As a boy, I was fortunate to be influenced by simple people who were possessed of simple wisdom. Except for my teachers and my minister, I don't think I knew anyone who was a college graduate. Most of my elders had, at best, finished the eighth grade. But although they didn't have formal training, they somehow got hold of some very down-to-earth insights on life.

I'm thinking just now of a man named Morris. I can't remember his first name, though I remember the names of his two older daughters! Perhaps it's because my parents always referred to him as "Brother Morris," in the style that marked warmhearted Iowa religion in the 1930s. One Sunday morning, apropos of something or other, he said, "Brother Ellsworth, just remember that religion is better caught than taught." He wasn't discounting Christian education; he had often taken his turn at teaching Sunday school. But he was sure that there are certain elements of life and faith that are best communicated through experience and influence.

I knew he was right. My instincts and my own experience told me so. And I have not found any substantial evidence to the contrary in the years I've spent in colleges, universities, and theological seminaries. The faith is better caught than taught.

Paul Holmer was for many years a distinguished member of the faculty of Yale University and of the Divinity School. He has all the credentials of the esteemed scholar: a doctor of philosophy degree from a leading university; honorary degrees from out-standing institutions in the United States and abroad; visiting lectureships in the United States, England, and the continent; author of several important books and contributions to a number of scholarly journals. In a word, Holmer is a scholar's scholar. One day a graduate student asked Holmer why he believed in God. The student meant it, I'm sure, as an intellectual challenge, and he expected an intellectual answer. But Holmer answered, "Because my mother told me."

He *caught* it. Mind you, his mother taught him about God, as did pastors and Sunday school teachers and a host of others. But essentially he was saying, "I caught it. I caught it from my mother."

That helps me understand the story of Moses. The book of Exodus tells us, in its lean, unadorned language, that a man of the house of Levi married a Levite woman and that they gave birth to a son. At the time, the Egyptians had decreed that all boy babies in the Hebrew community should be killed. But the mother of this baby saw that "he was a fine baby," so she hid him as long as she could. When she could hide him no longer, she worked with an older daughter, Miriam, to put the infant in a little basket in a quiet inlet of the Nile River. There he was discovered by Pharaoh's daughter, whereupon the sister slipped forward and volunteered to get a wet nurse from among the Hebrew women to nurse the child. So it was that the infant Moses was nursed by his own mother, though he was adopted by the Egyptian princess.

As the years went by, Moses grew up in the power, pomp, and panoply of a young prince. The people to whom he belonged by blood were living in slavery, while Moses was ensconced in luxurious comfort. By all logic, we would expect that he would have stayed in that comfortable, exclusive world. He had been reared and educated to be an Egyptian, and particularly, a member of the Egyptian ruling class, and it was highly advantageous for him to maintain that position.

Yet a day came when Moses "went out to his people and saw their forced labor" (Exodus 2:11). Suddenly he noticed one of the overseers beating one of his people, the people to whom he was tied by blood. He stepped forward in indignation and killed the overseer. With that act of earnest but perhaps misplaced idealism, the prince became a fugitive. Eventually he would become a great leader, deliverer, and lawgiver, but only after forty years as an exile, isolated in the back side of the desert.

Now the question is this: How is it that a person born to privilege became obsessed with a sense of justice? Since Moses belonged by right of adoption to the ruling party, why did he feel such instinctive sympathy for the downtrodden? Why didn't he shrug his shoulders, a la Marie Antoinette, and let the slaves eat cake? That is, where did he get such a concept of justice that he would rise up in righteous anger? And where did he get the conviction that his long-lost blood ties to the Hebrew slaves were more significant than his obvious, daily ties to the Egyptian throne and its power?

The Bible doesn't answer that question directly. I think the Bible often expects us to read between the lines, using basic common sense. Cecil B. DeMille did so in his epic film, *The Ten Commandments*. He concluded that Moses' mother had great and continuing influence on him, including that she gave him a sacred Hebrew garment that would always remind him of who he was and—more important—*whose* he was. I'm sure DeMille was on the right track. Perhaps that's because DeMille was a storyteller; and since the Hebrew scriptures were written by storytellers, he might well understand them better, at times, than do some professional theologians.

In any event, I'm struck by this: After Moses was born, everything having to do with his preservation is credited to his mother. See how it reads: *She* saw he was a fine baby, so *she* hid him; and when *she* could hide him no longer, *she* prepared a basket for him, and *she* placed him in the reeds of the Nile. I don't know where Moses' father was during all of this. He was probably bound in slavery; perhaps he had been executed. I only know that Moses' mother is at every step listed specifically as the acting party.

Through it all, she made her mark on Moses. We sometimes say half-poetically that some things in life we "drink in with our mother's milk." Well, I think Moses did that. As his mother held him to her bosom, I think she told him stories of the Lord God of Israel, reminding him that though the Hebrews were currently slaves, God didn't mean for them to remain in such a state. I venture even that she sang to him, as my mother sang to me, the songs of faith; and that in doing so, she planted in his soul, with words and rhythm, the pride of a people and the glory of their faith in God.

Now back to my question: How is it that Moses sensed, after years of privilege, that he should be concerned about those who were without privilege? How is it that though he was dressed and educated like an Egyptian, he couldn't forget that he was a Hebrew? If you had asked Moses, I think he might have answered, "Because my mother told me."

Of course, it works both ways. There's nothing magical about the word *mother*, just as there's nothing magical about such words as teacher, doctor, or minister. If you had asked Jacob, at another point in the Bible's story, why he lied to his father and cheated his brother, he could have answered rightly, "Because my mother told me."

Clearly, the same can be said for fathers. It's a title full of influence, but there's no guarantee that its power will be used for good. Shem, Ham, and Japheth could have caught faith from their father, Noah, because he was one of history's great heroes of faith, as the book of Hebrews notes (chap. 11). But they might also have caught from him an inclination to drunkenness (Genesis 9).

All of which simply says that there is untold power of influence in family: in mothers and fathers and siblings and aunts and uncles and grandparents. And also in all those persons who get close enough to us to teach us not only lessons that can be measured in a classroom test, but also lessons that are not always easy to verbalize. Sometimes they are the people who explain the differences between right and wrong and between the good and the best, and sometimes they are those who make us *want* to be good or those who give us a passion for what is best. Sometimes we call them mentors—a term that has its origin in Homer's *Odyssey,* in which a friend of Odysseus named Mentor is trusted to educate Odysseus' son. We may meet such persons in the classroom, but we are as likely to meet them in the workplace or the playing field; and above all, we meet them in the home and the neighborhood. Because so many of life's greatest commitments are established not only at the level of calculated logic but also at the level of inner conviction, we cannot fully explain why we believe so strongly, because our believing has been caught even more than it has been taught. This isn't to argue that the particular belief is irrational, but simply that the depth of the conviction goes beyond the sheer quality of its logical structures.

A generation ago William Warren Sweet said, "In certain realms of life emotion is a better guide than reason. And that is true in the higher realms more frequently than in the lower" (*Revivalism in America,* xiii). Sweet's statement has all the more impact when one remembers that he spent his long career in university education. Perhaps this is what we might call the wisdom of the heart. It is more than intuition, and surely more than untrammeled emotion. It is our peculiar human ability to perceive with the inner being, with a logic beyond logic, and with thinking that includes blood and sinew as well as brain. It is not infallible, of course—no more than the brain is! But in its own way it is more powerful than the brain because it involves so much more of the total person.

Leave some room in your life for the things you intuit. Not everything that matters can be fed into a computer or measured in a test tube. As a matter of fact, as Professor Sweet indicated, probably the most important things cannot. Peggy Noonan puts it in simple and straightforward style in her book, *What I Saw at the Revolution.* She was a writer with CBS News when she began to desire to become a speechwriter for President Ronald Reagan. But the odds were much against her. She had no connections in Washington, and she knew no one in the Republican Party. Furthermore, most people around Mr. Reagan were instinctively suspicious of someone associated with CBS News, particularly her division of that organization.

So she began doing anything she could to bring herself to the attention of the Republican Party, including "praying that God would open a door." She admits that this was asking for a small miracle. But she says, "I believe in miracles. The way I see it, life isn't flat and thin and 'realistic,' it's rich and full of mystery and surprise." She credits this to her Irish Catholic upbringing; and for her, that meant an ethnic neighborhood of a generation past, where Catholic piety was part of her own household and those of all the people with whom she associated day after day. She identifies herself, not as a particularly "good" Catholic, but as one whose life is so full of flaws that it makes "for real interesting confessions"; yet, with all of that, an "utterly believing" person.

These are the elements of a person whose religious convictions are more than logically constructed. They are bred
into a person's very being. Well, as you know if you're a
student of politics, Peggy Noonan not only got the job she
was seeking, she was the person ultimately responsible for
most of the memorable phrases in Mr. Reagan's speeches in
his second term, and in Mr. Bush's speeches during his
successful 1988 presidential candidacy. And everything
about Peggy's story indicates that her mother—and her
ethnic neighborhood and church—"told her." She "caught"
it. And to her credit, she is enough of an independent
thinker that she hasn't allowed secular society to take such
realities from her.

I want to leave two things with you. First, be very thankful
for the good you have caught from people—not only your
mother and father, if you have been so blessed, but any other
person who has touched your life at some point where you have
been ready to receive such a positive influence. God speaks to
us often, I'm sure, through the simple goodness (as if goodness
were ever really very simple!) we encounter in a variety of
people; and that goodness, and the nature of the relationship,
causes us to hear and to learn in a fashion that is much deeper
than pure logic.

Second, ponder how much someone—several
someones, no doubt!—may be catching from you. You
and I really have no idea what persons may be attending
to our words and our influence. And that includes some
who at a particular moment may respond with disdain or
skepticism. I'm not suggesting that you go about thinking
that people are finding gems of wisdom in your every
passing greeting, but I'm very sure that some people—
more than you think—are catching something from you.
Be sure that what they catch is good.

Because I'm thinking today of a woman, Moses' mother, and of
two very different men: Brother Morris, stocky little watch repair-
man with, at best, an eighth-grade education, reminding me that

some things "are better caught than taught," and an Ivy League scholar, who said, when he was asked why he believed in God, "Because my mother told me."

It's quite a marvel, this world in which we live. Far more of a marvel than sheer logic will ever fully explain.

CHAPTER *4*

Moses' Midlife Crisis

EXODUS 2:11-22: One day, after Moses had grown up, he went out to his people and saw their forced labor. He saw an Egyptian beating a Hebrew, one of his kinsfolk. He looked this way and that, and seeing no one he killed the Egyptian and hid him in the sand. When he went out the next day, he saw two Hebrews fighting; and he said to the one who was in the wrong, "Why do you strike your fellow Hebrew?" He answered, "Who made you a ruler and judge over us? Do you mean to kill me as you killed the Egyptian?" Then Moses was afraid and thought, "Surely the thing is known." When Pharaoh heard of it, he sought to kill Moses.

But Moses fled from Pharaoh. He settled in the land of Midian, and sat down by a well. The priest of Midian had seven daughters. They came to draw water, and filled the troughs to water their father's flock. But some shepherds came and drove them away. Moses got up and came to their defense and watered their flock. When they returned to their father Reuel, he said, "How is it that you have come back so soon today?" They said, "An Egyptian helped us against the shepherds; he even drew water for us and watered the flock." He said to his daughters, "Where is he? Why did you leave the man? Invite him to break bread." Moses agreed to stay with the man, and he gave Moses his daughter Zipporah in marriage. She bore a son, and he named him Gershom; for he said, "I have been an alien residing in a foreign land."

By popular definition, middle age is roughly the period between age forty and age sixty-five. I've come to raise the outer boundary a bit, because I reason that as long as there are people on either side of your age, you're still in the middle. I plan to stay middle-aged for a long time! In many parts of the world, the idea of "middle age" is a luxury, yet we Westerners don't necessarily see it as a blessing. We think it's a problem; and with our adeptness for glamorizing problems, we've given it a name: *midlife crisis.*

Several characteristics identify this problem. The most obvious is the condition of our bodies. We're no longer at our physical peak. We may still have plenty of stamina, and our contours may be generally acceptable, but—except for a few people like Nolan Ryan—we can no longer do the things we did at twenty or thirty. Women reach menopause sometime during this period; men don't have such a well-defined physical evidence of change, but studies indicate that the changes are there, nevertheless, and that in time science will be able to identify them more clearly.

Relationships change, too. Often married couples find themselves at some sort of crisis point: either the dramatic version that moves toward divorce, or the quiet despair of a union that is deteriorating into a kind of tired friendship. For those who are single and desiring marriage, the prospects are becoming less and less hopeful. For parents, it is the time when children are leaving home and the "empty-nest syndrome" is settling in.

Perhaps the worst characteristic of the midlife is a growing realization—and with it, a fear—that some cherished dreams will never come true. By middle age so much of the die of life has been cast that there is no returning. We realize that some dreams are now utterly impossible—like becoming Miss America, or being drafted by the NFL or the NBA. As for our more realistic dreams, some of them are now highly unlikely because of prior decisions, such as education or marriage or career choices.

In a sense, middle age is a foretaste of death. Death is the ultimate closing of doors; middle age is a preliminary closing. No wonder, then, that so many people at middle age begin a kind of frantic grasping for life and fulfillment. Sometimes it's healthy, like beginning a new regimen of exercise or study, or embarking on some new field of interest. Sometimes it's silly, like the woman who begins dressing like a teenager or the man who buys a car that he thinks will make him look like an adventuresome twenty-year-old. And sometimes it's destructive, as in those instances when people have a sexual fling or begin spending money with senseless abandon.

That's a midlife crisis. A person comes to a juncture where he or she feels that life, as known, is slipping away, and tries to catch it before it's gone. In many instances, it is also a time of personal revelation. In his book *Self-Renewal,* John Gardner said that by middle age most of us are "accomplished fugitives from ourselves." If the midlife crisis causes us to look at ourselves effectively, until we come to a more complete knowledge of ourselves, it can be the time when the self is redeemed and made wonderfully better.

Long, long ago—long before people talked about middle age and its problems—a man had a midlife crisis. His name was Moses. He was born to a family of Jewish slaves, and it was certain that his life would follow the same course, because all of his people had been slaves for several hundred years. In the good providence of God, however, he was adopted into an Egyptian family—and not just any Egyptian family, but the family of the king. He was adopted by the daughter of the pharaoh of all Egypt.

During his growing-up years and his young manhood, all Moses knew about life was privilege. He enjoyed the best the ancient world had to offer, and while that didn't include television or Nintendo games, it was still a pretty luxurious life. But then, the Bible says, there came a time when he "had grown up" (Exodus 2:11). The writer of Exodus doesn't say specifically how old he was, but we learn later, in the book of Acts, that this happened when Moses was forty years old (Acts 7:23). He was middle-aged.

Mind you, he didn't know he was middle-aged. They didn't have psychology, psychiatry, or *Reader's Digest,* so he didn't know what to call this point in life. But we know it was middle age by the way the experience hit Moses. After living all his life in the comfort, security, and exclusiveness of the palace, he went out to see what was happening to his ancestral people, the Jews. Of all things, he chose to watch them at "their forced labor" (Exodus 2:11). He was restless. That's a sure sign of middle age.

Then he saw that a slave master was beating one of the Hebrew slaves, and somehow it became clear to him that though he was a palace dweller, these slaves were really his own people. After glancing several directions to be sure no one was watching, he killed the slave master.

What provoked this dramatic, violent reaction from a man who for forty years had been trained to be sophisticated, restrained, and urbane in his conduct? Basically, as I tried to say in the foregoing chapter, he was now expressing convictions that had been instilled in him from the womb, convictions that he had caught from his mother. But why now, after so many years? Why did those inbred commitments lie dormant until this dramatic moment?

I think this is part of the peculiar chemistry of midlife. Mind you, it is a volatile, hazardous chemistry, with potential to blow up not only the subject's life, but also the lives of others nearby; that happened to Moses. But just as surely, this crisis time is the occasion of opportunity. I believe this is the moment when Moses is restless enough to be susceptible to an idealism that had been buried for years. At an earlier age, he was preoccupied with wealth and power; but at this midlife crisis, he has come to wonder if wealth and power are really worth that much; now he asks himself what he's doing with his life—what good and worthwhile thing is he doing that really matters? One needs an inner crisis to do such reevaluating, especially when life itself is very comfortable. And that kind of inner crisis is most likely to come at midlife, which is naturally a kind of uncomfortable period.

But, someone asks, where does God fit into all of this? Right where God always does: using the circumstances and common stuff of our lives for divine and eternal purposes. God, knowing our psyche better than anyone, speaks to us with particular poignancy at those times when we are most susceptible to the divine voice.

Unfortunately, Moses was seen, and the next day he had to flee the country. He ended up in Midian, where he married and became a shepherd. It wasn't much of a life compared with living in a palace. In fact, shepherding in that barren area wasn't much of a life compared with anything short of a concentration camp. But considering that it was the product of a midlife crisis, it could have been worse. He might easily have ended up wearing beads to the office and going to social occasions without wearing socks with his loafers!

After a while, he had a son. He named him Gershom, which means, "I have been an alien residing in a foreign land" (Exodus 2:22). This feeling that you don't belong anywhere and that you're a stranger is a sure sign of a person in midlife crisis—especially if you feel you're a stranger to yourself.

The whole story ends beautifully—not without pain, mind you, but beautifully. After many years—forty, the Bible says—Moses came to a transformational meeting with God. And though he felt he was poorly qualified, he went back to Egypt to become the deliverer of his people and eventually the historic lawgiver and the recipient of the Ten Commandments.

But it took forty years after that midlife crisis. One might even say that the crisis itself lasted for forty years. Not many of us want to spend so much of life in crisis, though in truth, many people do. Some people, Lord help them, spend most of their lives in a kind of wilderness, where they're looking for themselves or for satisfaction or purpose in living. They have a kind of lifelong midlife crisis. Compared with them, Moses' stretch of forty years doesn't sound too bad—especially in light of what followed.

Some Bible scholars look upon the forty years that Moses spent in the desert as a symbolic number. They explain that in the Bible, forty is often the number of testing or trial, or even of judgment. So it is that the Flood lasted for forty days and that Israel spent forty years in hopeless wandering and that Jesus fasted in the wilderness for forty days. One might also call it a character number, because in so many instances it is a number that reveals character or that puts character to the test.

Midlife in general is something like that. C. S. Lewis warned that middle age was "excellent campaigning weather for the Devil," whether as "the long, dull, monotonous years of middle-aged prosperity or middle-aged adversity." It's a testing time, whether people know it or not. The late E. Stanley Jones wrote an epic book on conversion. In it he said that most people need a rebirth in their forties "on general principles." Unfortunately, not everyone experiences such a rebirth. Many people seem instead to accommodate themselves to the period. Instead of seeking and finding a new fullness in God, they settle for a new car or a larger mortgage or a Caribbean cruise or a fling.

But a midlife crisis doesn't have to be all bad. Actually, it can well be the very door of opportunity. Consider Moses. That the author describes these events as happening after "he had grown up" is itself significant. It's only as we're ready to cope with a crisis that we give evidence of maturity. It was good that Moses was stirred by the suffering of his ancestral people. If you can grow comfortable with the suffering that is in the world, you're a long way from maturity.

I hate to think what Moses would have become if he hadn't gotten upset that day. He probably would have spent the rest of his life eating ceremonial dinners, cutting ribbons for the dedication of new pyramids, and getting fat. Instead, he got to spend the next forty years of his life tending sheep and the last forty leading a group of frequently ungrateful, complaining slaves into freedom and to the edge of the promised land. And when it was all over, God told him to come home by a special route, because he had done a good job. Incidentally—and everything is incidental to God's telling you that you've done a good job—he went down in history as the first great emancipator and as the lawyer who negotiated the Ten Commandments. And it all came about through a crisis, a midlife crisis for a sated forty-year-old!

All of us have more midlives than show on the calendar. Midlife, spiritually speaking, is a state of the soul. It can happen when you're twelve or thirteen—in fact, that's one of the very best times, which is why we have so many teenage conversions. It can also happen when you're thirty-five, sixty-five, or eighty-two. It is especially likely to happen when a first baby is born, or when we've lost a job or a friend, or when a marriage is in crisis. A midlife crisis is much more than a particular birthday.

Of course it doesn't really matter when it comes. What matters is what we do with it. We can grow used to it and make peace with it, so to speak, or we can let it destroy us. Or, by God's grace, we can use it as an occasion for meeting God and for allowing the Holy Spirit to transform all that we are.

If you're at such a crisis in your life—midlife by the calendar or simply by the juxtaposition of events—don't be afraid of it. That place where pain and confusion meet can become the junction of God's opportunity. You may have to spend a little time there; how long depends pretty much on you. But even if you spend a bit too long there, take it from me, that's not all bad. Not if, in the end, you come closer to God and to God's purposes in your life.

Take a good look at Moses on that day when he stepped out of his palace, forty years old and naive as a plum. He had no idea he was entering a midlife crisis. And he couldn't have dreamed what was ahead of him: flight from the law, years of tending sheep, more years of struggling with difficult people.

But with it all, the glory of God! The wonderful, ineffable, majestic glory of God! And it all began with a midlife crisis.

Patron Saint
of the Minority Report

NUMBERS 13:1-3, 25-33: The LORD said to Moses, "Send men to spy out the land of Canaan, which I am giving to the Israelites; from each of their ancestral tribes you shall send a man, every one a leader among them." So Moses sent them from the wilderness of Paran, according to the command of the LORD, all of them leading men among the Israelites. . . .

At the end of forty days they returned from spying out the land. And they came to Moses and Aaron and to all the congregation of the Israelites in the wilderness of Paran, at Kadesh; they brought back word to them and to all the congregation, and showed them the fruit of the land. And they told him, "We came to the land to which you sent us; it flows with milk and honey, and this is its fruit. Yet the people who live in the land are strong, and the towns are fortified and very large; and besides, we saw the descendants of Anak there. The Amalekites live in the land of the Negeb; the Hittites, the Jebusites, and the Amorites live in the hill country; and the Canaanites live by the sea, and along the Jordan."

But Caleb quieted the people before Moses, and said, "Let us go up at once and occupy it, for we are well able to overcome it." Then the men who had gone up with him said, "We are not able to go up against this people, for they are stronger than we." So they brought to the Israelites an unfavorable report of the land that they had spied out, saying, "The land that we have gone through as spies is a land that devours its inhabitants; and all the people that we saw in it are of great size. There we saw the Nephilim (the Anakites come from the Nephilim); and to ourselves we seemed like grasshoppers, and so we seemed to them."

Once upon a time there was a man who had the courage to be in the minority. For a while it looked as if it would cost him his life, but in the end it was his minority courage which made him outlive his contemporaries. In fact, he has outlived them to this very day, so that his name is still remembered, while those who voted with the majority are long forgotten.

His name was Caleb, and you'll find his story in the Hebrew scriptures in the book of Numbers. You may have the impression that Numbers isn't a very exciting book, but Caleb's story is not only one of the most exciting ever written, it is also one of the most instructive.

When the Jewish people escaped the slavery of Egypt centuries ago, it was with the promise that God would give them a land of their own. It was to be a land of abundance, described as flowing with milk and honey—which is a way of saying that it would have not only life's necessities, but also some luxuries. In time, the Jews were within striking distance of the land that had been promised to them. They selected a committee to explore the land, to determine their best course of action. It was a good committee. All of them were leaders, each representing one of the twelve tribes of Israel. The committee lacked female representation, unfortunately, but that was typical of the times.

At its best, a committee is an ingenious idea. It gives the opportunity of acting with the wisdom of five or seven or a dozen persons rather than of one. Every committee is an exercise in democracy. One might say that the writer of Proverbs was endorsing committee action when he said:

> Without counsel, plans go wrong,
>   but with many advisers they succeed.
>
> (PROVERBS 15:22)

Something special can happen when several minds interact; one good mind, brushing against another, will often set up such intellectual friction that a full-blown fire is kindled.

Unfortunately, however, committees seldom fulfill their potential. Any of us who have given interminable hours of our lives in committee meetings will testify to that. Often it's because members of a committee don't prepare for the meeting, each one assuming that others will carry the weight, or perhaps thinking that something magic will happen just because half a dozen unprepared people have gotten together.

But usually there's a greater problem. Committees tend to make people cautious. That's why committees almost never produce startling insights or dramatic action. They tend, even more than individuals, to follow the path of least resistance. A certain lethargy is native to committees. They feel obligated to be ponderous and deliberative. Often they bow under the weight of their own impressiveness. Some committees seem to feel that it's their responsibility to cut an idea down to manageable size. And in the process, they often leave the idea bleeding and dying. No one can estimate how many brilliant ideas have been born in committees, or brought to committees by imaginative members, only to be molded at last, by committee action, into a tame, routine, dull, colorless thing. Who can say how many committee mountains have strained for months to bring forth a molehill idea?

Israel's Committee of Twelve made a forty-day study. They fulfilled their assignment—a rather dangerous one, frankly—and they did it well. They examined a large area of the land, and brought back samples of grapes, pomegranates, and figs. The land was rich! A cluster of grapes was so large that two men were needed to carry it back on a pole between them, as Exhibit A of their study.

When the committee returned, it was greeted with great excitement. "The land flows with milk and honey," they said, "and here is a sample of its fruit." But at that point, the majority report turned sour. "Yet the people who live in the land," they continued, "are strong, and the towns are fortified and very large; and besides, we saw the descendants of Anak there" (Numbers 13:28). Then they proceeded to list other names that terrified them—Amalekites, Hittites, Jebusites, Amorites, Canaanites—names that today sound like parties to a comic opera, but to the Committee (or at least to its majority) they were a litany of despair.

As I read the report in Numbers, I can almost feel the silence settling over the gathered throng. Children who had jumped and danced at the sight of the fruit of the promised land now slipped into their mothers' skirts. Men bowed their heads and their shoulders sagged. Here and there in the crowd, women sobbed and old men shook their heads in resignation. These were people who had never known anything but slavery, and some of them were now thinking that they were never intended to be more. Slowly, an unhappy murmur began to build.

At this point, our man Caleb began his minority report. He quieted the people, then said, "Let us go up at once and occupy it, for we are well able to overcome it" (Numbers 13:30). Immediately the majority—ten of the twelve Committee members!—answered, "We can't attack those people; they are stronger than we are. The land we explored devours those living in it. All the people we saw there are of great size. We seemed like grasshoppers in our own eyes, and we looked the same to them" (Numbers 13:31*b*, 32*b*, 33*b* NIV).

Did you notice the inconsistency in that majority report? It would be hilarious if it weren't so pathetic. The Committee said, on the one hand, that the land devoured its inhabitants; and in the next, they declared that the inhabitants were men of great stature, veritable giants! You can't have it both ways, can you? But they were painfully correct in one specific. They said they felt like grasshoppers in their own eyes and looked the same to their potential enemies. It's very clear that when a person feels like a grasshopper, other people will soon come to the same conclusion. The image we carry of ourselves is usually, eventually, the image others get. Each of us is three people: what we are, what we perceive ourselves to be, and what others see us to be. And what others see us to be is usually closer to what we perceive ourselves to be than to what we are.

A cry rose up in the camp. The people wept all that night. Then they began to murmur against Moses and Aaron, the leaders of the fledgling nation. They said they wished they had died in Egypt—the land where they had been slaves, and from which they were so glad to be delivered that they had sung like angels upon their escape—or that they had died in the wilderness in which they were now traveling. Then, suddenly, someone said, "Let's choose a captain and go back to Egypt." Back to slavery! Can you imagine that?

Moses and Aaron fell on their faces, and Joshua and Caleb, who had offered the minority report, rent their clothing, which was a demonstration in the ancient Middle East of grief and shame. I don't know if Joshua was silent at the first reporting, but he was one of the twelve spies, and he was the only one who at last joined Caleb in the minority report.

Caleb and Joshua appealed to the people. They said that the land was good beyond description, perhaps pointing again to the collection of fruit. And it could be theirs, they insisted, if the Lord delighted in them. It was land, they said, which flowed with milk and honey. Then they pushed the crucial point: *The Lord is with us, so we have no reason to fear the enemy.*

So how did the people respond to this courageous cry from the minority? They decided to stone them! They wanted to stone Caleb and Joshua for believing and hoping, and they would choose instead to return to their former condition of slavery, or to die enroute.

It sounds irrational, doesn't it? But unbelief makes a person irrational. There's a popular idea that insists faith is irrational, and no doubt there are instances where faith is so misused. But unbelief is far more irrational. It makes us our own worst enemies. When we live with doubt and fear, we take sides against ourselves. What could be more irrational than that? Only this: that unbelief also makes us line up against God. Now *that,* believe me, is irrational!

So the minority said, "We can do it," and the majority answered, "We'll never make it." And of course both were right. In the next forty years, the majority proved they were right, and it wasn't hard, either. All they had to do was to do nothing, and most of us are good at that. But the minority also proved, in a little more than forty years, that *they* were right. Really, finally, wonderfully right—a rightness that proved how wrong the majority had actually been.

I have a great deal of regard for minority reports. Take American history, for instance. The venerable American historian John Hicks said that when the American Revolution began, those who wanted freedom from England were doubtless a minority. As for those who really, measurably supported the Revolution, they were an almost minuscule minority. During the winter at Valley Forge, Washington's army was a bare two thousand men, and the people of America weren't willing to pay taxes to support the cause. We moderns enjoy what the world hails as American freedom because of a minority, and the dogged devotion with which they held to their minority position.

The church has a debt to its minority positions, too. The genius of Catholicism has been its readiness to accept new Orders, like the Jesuits and the Franciscans, who have revitalized the whole body by their vigorous minority energy. The genius of Protestantism is the spiritual renewal which has repeatedly occurred through the influence of minority movements. We may not agree with everything that has been said and done by all the splinter groups in Protestantism, but we owe them more than we will ever fully realize, and surely more than we will acknowledge. When Protestantism had lost sight of the role of faith in physical and emotional healing, Christian Science made it an issue. Seventh Day Adventists have kept us alert to the issue of religious liberty and to a concern for the Sabbath. Pentecostal bodies have reawakened us to the importance of the Holy Spirit. If ever the day comes when Protestantism, or most of it, is united in one large denomination, that denomination had better have room for vigorous minority reports. If it doesn't, little churches will soon break off from the one big church. And if I happen to be around at that time, you'll probably find me among them.

I'm not giving a blanket endorsement to minority voices. My case is for the responsible minority. I hold no brief for people who are in a minority simply because they want to be different, nor for those who are working out their neuroses in some religious or political expression. Some minority movements are thoughtless and destructive, and many can see no farther than their own small agenda, until they think their little agenda is the business of the whole universe. Nevertheless, what organization or what nation can dare to close its mind to the voice of minor segments within its group? And who can say what potential melody may be found in even the unseemly dissonance of one apparently irrational voice?

The people were preparing to stone Caleb and Joshua because they could not hear the melody in their minority report. Then God intervened. Judgment was pronounced on the faithless nation. Not one of the generation that had seen the wonders of the Lord in delivering them from Egypt and had now retreated from entering the promised land would ever enter that place. They would wander in the wilderness until all of their adult generation had passed away. Of the original group, only Caleb and Joshua would ever enter the inheritance which had been promised to all the people.

So for forty years the Israelites wandered in the wilderness. Some say the number is symbolic: a matter of wandering a year for each day the Committee had spent in its research of the promised land. Others point out that forty years is essentially the time span for an adult generation. Still others argue that the wilderness in which they were supposed to have wandered wasn't really large enough to contain them for such a long period.

Those who raise this latter argument know geography better than they know human nature. I've known people who lived all their lives without really leaving the "block" in which they were born: not because they were happy in that block, but because they didn't have the gumption—faith, if you please—to rise up and find a new life. And I've known churches that stagnated, slowly dying, for a whole generation without taking a step forward for God because—like Israel—they had to wait for a generation to die off before they could hope to move ahead. The truth is, it would have been a miracle if the Israelites had gone into the promised land as long as that negative generation was living— much more of a miracle, really, than their wandering for forty years.

As for Caleb, our saint of the minority report, he saw the promised land. Of course he did! How could it be otherwise? His whole generation died in the wilderness, but he walked in the promised land. Caleb's minority report was the product of his faith. He saw the land after forty years, and possessed it, because he saw it—and saw it in a way ten of his companions could not—when he was part of that Committee exploration forty years before. Caleb looked at life through the eyes of faith, and as a result, he saw much more than others saw. Consequently, he got more out of life than others got.

People of faith are always making minority reports. The world around them goes with the times, the fads, the headlines—and yes, the polls! But those who choose to follow God in faith always have sight of a higher goal than the latest stock market report, society column, or public opinion sampling. They somehow see the purposes of God, even when the noise and bluster of society would seem to drown them out. No wonder then that one day they get to the promised land! When you have faith, you're not willing to die in the wilderness. You've seen God and God's will, and you intend to follow on until that eternal goal has been reached.

And you'll be there when it happens. You can count on it.

CHAPTER 6

Tragic Son, Tragic Father

JUDGES 11:1-6, 30-35: Now Jephthah the Gileadite, the son of a prostitute, was a mighty warrior. Gilead was the father of Jephthah. Gilead's wife also bore him sons; and when his wife's sons grew up, they drove Jephthah away, saying to him, "You shall not inherit anything in our father's house; for you are the son of another woman." Then Jephthah fled from his brothers and lived in the land of Tob. Outlaws collected around Jephthah and went raiding with him.

After a time the Ammonites made war against Israel. And when the Ammonites made war against Israel, the elders of Gilead went to bring Jephthah from the land of Tob. They said to Jephthah, "Come and be our commander, so that we may fight with the Ammonites." . . .

And Jephthah made a vow to the LORD, and said, "If you will give the Ammonites into my hand, then whoever comes out of the doors of my house to meet me, when I return victorious from the Ammonites, shall be the LORD's, to be offered up by me as a burnt offering." So Jephthah crossed over to the Ammonites to fight against them; and the LORD gave them into his hand. He inflicted a massive defeat on them from Aroer to the neighborhood of Minnith, twenty towns, and as far as Abelkeramim. So the Ammonites were subdued before the people of Israel.

Then Jephthah came to his home at Mizpah; and there was his daughter coming out to meet him with timbrels and with dancing. She was his only child; he had no son or daughter except her. When he saw her, he tore his clothes, and said, "Alas, my daughter! You have brought me very low; you have become the cause of great trouble to me. For I have opened my mouth to the LORD, and I cannot take back my vow."

Some of the most fascinating and instructive persons in the Bible are hidden away in places where we might easily miss them. Give that person a name that is virtually unknown in our time, and he or she is still more likely to be missed. Then, to cap it, let the person's story be of a kind that is far removed from our time and culture, and we'll almost surely miss the acquaintance.

I don't want that to happen to Jephthah. For thirty years or more, he has been one of my favorite biblical characters. If you know his story, you may think it perverse of me to be drawn to such a person. You may even do some amateur psychologizing, to see if you can understand why I feel as I do.

His story seems to be a classic tragedy. He began life as a tragic son and ended it as a tragic father. For me, he symbolizes those persons whose lives seem stalked by tragedy, as if they were its chosen victims. From birth to adult life and finally to death, their path is a series of confusions and pains. And perhaps that isn't too surprising, because in the reproductive strategy of our world, like begets like; so why shouldn't tragedy produce tragedy, and still more tragedy, until the victim concludes that life itself is just one pain after another? See how the writer of Judges introduces Jephthah to us: "Jephthah the Gileadite was a mighty warrior. His father was Gilead; his mother was a prostitute" (Judges 11:1 NIV). The biblical writers rarely waste words. They give us the data in quite stark terms and leave it to us to interpret the implications.

But the next six words give our imaginations room to work: "Gilead's wife also bore him sons." Gilead was apparently a person of some economic substance, so he took the baby Jephthah into his home. Let us give him credit for that. And let's give credit, too, to his wife, that she accepted this responsibility, because it must surely have been an unwelcome one. She could hardly help resenting the boy; after all, he was a daily reminder of her husband's infidelity, and now she was left to bear much of the brunt of it. We don't know Gilead's feelings. He may well have adored the boy. Still, Jephthah was a living embodiment of Gilead's transgressions, so that any time Gilead might think he could forget his earlier indiscretions, the boy was a reminder. A conscience is exceedingly valuable, but you may hate to see it put its feet under your table three times a day.

As for the half-brothers, I think they must have sensed the strangeness in Jephthah long before they knew the story behind his birth. Our human instincts are peculiar in such regards; we so often intuit what no one has verbalized. I think therefore that they must have formed a childhood league against this brother who was "different." And of course that increased Jephthah's differentness. When people treat us as if we are odd, it's very difficult not to fulfill their opinion of us.

What went through Jephthah's mind in those growing-up years? Once he knew his heritage, did he curse his mother's profession and his father's passion? And did he compensate by proving, in very boyish ways, that he was stronger, more daring, more careless of danger than his half-brothers? Did he sometimes tell them that he would someday outshine them all? But then, in the darkness of falling asleep, did he lose heart and curse the God who permitted his conception?

Inevitably, the day came when Jephthah's brothers drove him from the house. You knew they would. "You shall not inherit anything in our father's house," they said, "for you are the son of another woman" (Judges 11:2). It's sad, isn't it, that we humans can be so unkind in rejecting someone for matters which are not of that person's doing! So Jephthah fled, probably rejoicing that he was getting free of this hostile atmosphere, and he settled in the land of Tob.

But he was a leader. It may have been in his blood, or it may have been the drive that sometimes inhabits an immigrant or a slum-dweller. Before long he had gathered a group of men around him—the New Revised Standard Version calls them "outlaws," and the older Revised Standard Version "worthless fellows." It was the kind of crowd only a powerful, instinctive leader could have melded into a unity, and Jephthah did it. They became raiders, fearsome soldiers of fortune.

Life takes some ironic twists. In time the Israelites faced war with a neighboring nation, and they lacked the kind of military leader who could give them a shot at victory. So they sent a delegation to Jephthah, pleading with him to lead their forces. Jephthah was quick to remind them that they had once cast him out; I can't say I blame him! If he were to return, he said, and was successful in battle, they must make him head over the people. The delegation was desperate enough that they accepted his conditions. After all, the alternative was subjection to the despised Ammonites, so Jephthah didn't look so bad.

Jephthah must have been a brilliantly able man. Perhaps the mottled circumstances of his life had built strengths others might not easily have cultivated. With remarkable statesmanship, he tried first to avoid war by a series of conferences with the Ammonites. But eventually it was clear that no reconciliation could be had. As his people organized for battle, Jephthah made a vow to God. "If you will give the Ammonites into my hand," he pledged, "then whoever comes out of the doors of my house to meet me, when I return victorious from the Ammonites, shall be the LORD's, to be offered up by me as a burnt offering" (Judges 11:30-31).

It was a strange, violent contract. Some theologians feel that Jephthah thought the first thing to come from his house would be an animal, but the language of the vow seems to indicate that he expected to sacrifice a fellow human being. Probably he thought that the person coming first would be one of his servants or some other associate, which meant he was prepared to take the life of some person whose devotion to him was so great that he or she would lead the way in loving celebration. However one views it, the vow is incomprehensible in our day and culture. Many people still bargain with God, promising that they will go to church faithfully if they recover from surgery, or that they will give a certain sum to the church if they succeed in a business deal. But even those who engage in such divine speculation couldn't imagine vowing a human sacrifice.

Let me make clear that the Hebrew scriptures never approved of human sacrifices. Such procedures were fairly common among some of Israel's neighbors, but they were strictly forbidden to the Jews. But it isn't unusual for people to pick up the sins of their neighbors; as a matter of fact, it's astonishing to see how quickly that reprehensible conduct observed can become conduct copied. Jephthah was a rugged man. He had struggled for every success he had gotten. He believed in winning; he might well have said that "winning is the only thing." A person with such a passion for winning often feels the price is almost incidental. And that is as true in politics, sports, and business as it is in the world of the military.

Well, Jephthah won. He gained a magnificent victory and returned home exultant. But as he approached his home, the first to come out of his house to meet him was his daughter. The sacred writer makes a point with stark pathos: "She was his only child; he had no son or daughter except her" (Judges 11:34). She came playing the timbrels and dancing, rejoicing in her father's victory, proud of his achievement. She was all of his life, just on the edge of womanhood, a beautiful thing; and she adored her father, so that his victory was now her greatest pride.

As the girl ran to Jephthah, it was as if the heavens fell. The warrior tore off his clothes and wept. "Alas, my daughter!" he cried. "You have brought me very low; you have become the cause of great trouble to me. For I have opened my mouth to the LORD, and I cannot take back my vow" (Judges 11:35). You and I have several reactions to his statement. We want to tell him that it is not his daughter who has brought him low, but his own foolish vow. We want to grasp him by his armor and tell him that God would honor him more in the breaking of this vow than in his keeping it. But Jephthah is all of a piece; he is a man of severe commitments. Life has been to him a pattern of high stakes, and now it has simply risen to the ultimate measure.

This is a strange story, but perhaps the strangest thing about it is its commonness. We know this story well, you and I, for we have seen it played out any number of times. We know Jephthah—not in his warrior garb, but in a Brooks Brothers suit. He may belong to your neighborhood bridge group; perhaps you've lent him your power mower. I'm not speaking, of course, of Jephthah the son of a harlot, but of Jephthah who sacrifices his daughter in winning a battle. Tragic man, he sacrificed what was dearest to him in order to win something that had little meaning without that dearest thing. You know him well.

Let me dare to spell it out. Sometimes it's the businessman whose life is a continual flurry of activity: meetings, plane trips, conferences, executive meetings. "You have to make it while you can," he explains. "I have three kids to get through college. I want them to have the advantages I never got." But when Jephthah brings home his greatest triumph, he sometimes discovers that he has sacrificed his son or his daughter to get it.

Nor is this kind of sacrifice limited to fathers. I remember a young woman whose life was already severely complicated by bad choices. When I asked her to trace her troubles back to some starting point, she spoke sadly—and with no real malice—of a mother who "was never around when I needed her. Especially when I was in my midteens, and wanted so much to talk, just talk." The mother was busy about good things. Perhaps winning battles for other people, or for good causes.

Since this story is so commonplace, why are we so shocked when we read it in the scripture? True, Jephthah is more primitive, but he's no more at fault than a million modern parents. Jephthah didn't know when he left for battle that with that vow he would lose his daughter, the only thing that really mattered to him.

Jephthah was the leader of Israel for six years after that. He won other triumphs, including the peculiar "shibboleth" battle. But the thing he loved most was gone.

Men and women cheered, of course, when Jephthah passed by in parade, and common folks envied him. "He's a big man," they told their children. "Probably the greatest general since Joshua." And people who knew him only from a distance said, "He's got it made. Lucky fellow."

But Jephthah himself, on quiet nights when there was no state activity, would watch while embers slowly died in a fire and would ask the meaning of it all. Why had he been born in such tragedy, son of a prostitute? And why had he lost his daughter in still more tragedy? Tragic son, tragic father! Why had tragedy dogged his private life, even while he won success in his public life?

As I said earlier, we shouldn't really be surprised that tragedy begets tragedy. That's the law of genetics, is it not, that like begets like? Not only do dogs beget dogs, and people beget people; poverty begets poverty, and wealth, wealth. So of course, tragedy can be expected to produce still more tragedy. We experience it frequently on a smaller scale: When we suffer some indignity or reversal, we're thrown off balance; so when the next issue comes along, we're still more susceptible to defeat. Tragedy, of whatever size, is likely to reproduce itself. And when a person's life begins in tragedy, it isn't surprising that worse tragedy follows. As a matter of fact, logic expects it.

Except for grace. I wish I could have told Jephthah about grace. I wish, especially, that I could have intercepted him in the days before his daughter's death, to say that a tragic son can become a blessed father.

I wish I could have told him of a friend of mine, a minister, who dared not long before his retirement to tell his congregation in a Father's Day sermon of the grace of God in his life. He recalled that his own father had been consumed by addiction. So his father never gave him a hug, a kiss, even a word of affirmation; his father never participated in any important event of his life or offered one gift in all of his childhood and adolescence. When his father died, my friend officiated at his funeral, and only one person was there besides the six children.

With such a tragic, paternally loveless upbringing, my friend was set up to repeat the process. Instead, however, he and his wife have brought up a beautiful family, all of them strong, loving adults. The two sons are ministers. By the grace of God, the "genetic process" of tragedy begetting tragedy was broken.

I pondered it again not long ago as I officiated at a baptism. I have seen hundreds of proud and dedicated parents through the years, but—perhaps because I knew their story—these parents stood out. As I looked at the father, I reflected on what I knew of him. His own father had left when he was an infant, and he had seen him only once, when he was in his teens. But the grace of God, communicated through his mother and some friends and his church, had made all the difference. Now he was breaking the cycle of tragedy.

Perhaps the reason I am so fascinated by the Jephthah story is that I believe the tragedy was avoidable. It didn't have to be repeated. I believe this because I believe God has a lively commitment to our human struggle. Graciously, God brings new factors into the chemistry of our lives which can make the bitter waters sweet and cause the distresses and reversals of life to become productive. Such is the nature of God; to build where life is a shambles, and to redeem when all seems lost.

So I believe that, philosophical genetics aside, the tragic son–tragic father syndrome is not an inviolable one. Life does not have to breed tragedy from tragedy. God, who is gracious and omnipotent, can bring good from the womb of sorrow—if, that is, we will work with God to that end.

And so it shall be that the Jephthahs who are born in tragedy shall come to live in peace, and die in the love of God. That, in some small but crucial and intimate measure, is what we mean by the grace of God. And that's how, at last, the son of tragedy can become the father of blessing.

CHAPTER 7

Honey in the Lion

JUDGES 14:5-14: Then Samson went down with his father and mother to Timnah. When he came to the vineyards of Timnah, suddenly a young lion roared at him. The spirit of the LORD rushed on him, and he tore the lion apart barehanded as one might tear apart a kid. But he did not tell his father or his mother what he had done. Then he went down and talked with the woman, and she pleased Samson. After a while he returned to marry her, and he turned aside to see the carcass of the lion, and there was a swarm of bees in the body of the lion, and honey. He scraped it out into his hands, and went on, eating as he went. When he came to his father and mother, he gave some to them, and they ate it. But he did not tell them that he had taken the honey from the carcass of the lion.

His father went down to the woman, and Samson made a feast there as the young men were accustomed to do. When the people saw him, they brought thirty companions to be with him. Samson said to them, "Let me now put a riddle to you. If you can explain it to me within the seven days of the feast, and find it out, then I will give you thirty linen garments and thirty festal garments. But if you cannot explain it to me, then you shall give me thirty linen garments and thirty festal garments." So they said to him, "Ask your riddle; let us hear it." He said to them,

"Out of the eater came
   something to eat.
Out of the strong came
   something sweet."

But for three days they could not explain the riddle.

I've often wondered why we find so much pleasure in riddles. They are part of every culture since ancient times. Most of us are introduced to them in elementary school, as likely from some classmate as from a teacher—and as likely on the playground as in the classroom. They're the stuff of parties for some people, and you can buy them by the bookful.

I've concluded that we love the riddles we make up because they are more manageable than the riddles life itself serves us. Alexander Pope, the eighteenth-century essayist, said that we humans are ourselves "the glory, jest and riddle of the world." No wonder we riddles play with riddles!

Many centuries ago, a young man constructed a riddle for his own enjoyment and for the mystifying of some new companions. I've come to feel that his riddle is itself a surprising answer to one of our most frustrating human riddles.

His name was Samson, and he wasn't the kind of person you would expect to provide material for philosophical discussions. We remember him mainly for his legendary strength—and also, come to think of it, for his equally legendary weakness. His ability to dismember small armies with his bare hands or with nothing more than the jawbone of an ass has made his name synonymous with physical strength. But his inability to restrain his interest in women has left him, as well, with a reputation as a person who was shorn of his strength.

But that's another story. I'm thinking just now of a day when Samson set out to court a young woman in a distant community. As he traveled through the wild, rugged area, he encountered a young lion. With his phenomenal strength, "He tore the lion apart barehanded as one might tear apart a kid" (Judges 14:6).

Some time later he was traveling the same road, and he came upon the carcass of the lion. But now he found that a swarm of bees had taken residence there. In that barren area, where there were very few hollow trees, wild bees often established colonies in the carcass of an animal; the tough, dry hide provided a perfect home.

So the carcass was now rich with honey. Samson scooped out a generous supply and went on his way, eating as he went. He even gave some to his parents, although he didn't tell them its source. Perhaps he thought their tastes might be more delicate than his!

Then it was time for his wedding. In those days and in that culture, one of the amusements in the course of a wedding celebration was for a groom to test his fellows with a riddle. And of course some wagers were involved. Samson drew on his own recent experience, and presented this riddle:

> Out of the eater came something to eat.
> Out of the strong came something sweet.
>
> (JUDGES 14:14)

The men in the bridal party weren't able to come up with the answer. Not, at least, until they got it from the bride. But that, too, is another matter. Our interest just now is in the parable that is hidden in Samson's story. He found nourishment—life—in that which had threatened to take life from him. The lion was by nature an eater, but out of his carcass came something to eat. Samson found sweetness in what might have been his destruction. He found *honey in the lion.*

Blessed are those who learn that there is honey in the lion! Let there be no question about it: On our human journey we're sure to encounter any number of lions. Not the kind of wild beast Samson met, but nonetheless fierce. Indeed, it's possible that Samson's lion would be easier to deal with (or even run from!) than the lions you and I have to meet.

Some of life's lions are capable of destroying us; others simply maul and maim us, leaving us marked for the rest of life. Some lions challenge the whole populace—like war and economic depression. Those who live in especially rugged places have to meet the lions of violence, poverty, and constant rejection. Those who live with such dangers no doubt envy others, not knowing that the outwardly comfortable and self-possessed usually have their own lions—social pressure, job pressure, nerves, tension, and the menace of superficiality. And every one of us, whatever road we travel, has to meet such terrors as sickness, bereavement, death, disappointment, disillusionment. Every human being, whatever his or her road of life, must face some lions.

Some, faced by their lion, simply give up. "Why me?" they say; or, "Why must life be like this?" Others become bitter. They clench a fist at life and take on the nature of the lion itself, turning to prey upon and devour others, just as they have been preyed upon and attacked. "Life's tough," they say, "and only the tough survive. Get the other guy before he gets you." They live by the rule of David Harum, the popular fictional character from earlier in this century: "Do to the other person what he'd like to do to you, but you do it first." In a world which has its lions, they add to its ravenous, destructive quality.

But others discover the secret of Samson's riddle. In the eater, they find something to eat. In the strong, they find something sweet. They find honey in the lion.

Believe me, there is always honey in the lion, if only we will look for it, demand it, contend for it, love it! Here is one of the most astonishing, unexpected, and miraculous facts of the life we know: that we can so often harvest good out of the destruction and brutality of our experiences. I don't want to overstate the case, yet I must speak a strong word: Sometimes the honey in the lion is the very best, the very sweetest, that life will ever offer.

Consider what most people would agree is the worst of the lions, at least among those lions which involve much of the human race—war. In a sense, nothing good can be said for war; it is a roaring, bestial, destructive thing, reckless of life and scornful of pain. Yet there was honey in World War II. Scientists confess that we made greater progress in the development of medicine during those years than would have happened in a whole generation of peace, especially in the development of antibiotics. Havelock Ellis, the British author and psychologist, said that there is nothing war has ever achieved that we could not better achieve without it. Theoretically, yes; but the hard facts show otherwise. The war made rapid medical progress absolutely essential, and progress we did.

And consider poverty. The sidewalk philosopher might say, "I've been rich, and I've been poor, and I can tell you that I'd rather be rich." Well, I've never been rich, but I've been poor and I've also been comfortable, and—yes, I prefer being comfortable. But I'm thankful for the years of poverty, in my growing up in the Great Depression. A Sunday school class asked me to identify the greatest influences in my life. The first two were predictable: my faith in God, and my parents. But I didn't need long to add a third: growing up poor. Yes, I have many painful memories of those years—but far more good memories. I recall so many fine people, so much learning about human courage, so many simple pleasures. I don't want anyone to be poor, yet I wish that, in the midst of more comfortable living, we could still get some of the special beauties that I found in poverty.

History has so many dramatic stories of individuals who have found honey in the lion. The name of Demosthenes is almost synonymous with oratory. But Demosthenes had to wrestle with a lion. He had grand thoughts and phrases, but he also had a harsh voice, weak lungs, and an awkward manner. What a tragedy to have music in your soul and the hunger to share it with others, but to have a demon in your manner which would make people snicker when you try to share the beauty you feel! But Demosthenes recited as he climbed steep hills; he practiced speaking with pebbles in his mouth in order to build clarity of speech; and he spoke against the roar of the ocean to strengthen his vocal powers. I'm sure, as one professor has said, that a good college advisory system would never have allowed Demosthenes to major in public address. But Demosthenes became the historic symbol of oratory. He found honey in his lion.

You know John Milton's story. Blind at middle age, he struggled with despair:

> When I consider how my light is spent
> E're half my days in this dark world and wide,

and concluded that his gift was lodged with him "useless." Yet he took solace in his faith. And in the years that followed, in his darkness, Milton wrote his greatest works, *Paradise Lost* and *Paradise Regained.* Likewise, John Bunyan wrote literature's most notable allegory, *Pilgrim's Progress,* not in the comfort of a scholar's study but in a prison cell. Beethoven envisioned a career as a concert pianist, but his growing deafness drove him into composition. Most of his greatest works were composed as his hearing failed, and his immortal Ninth Symphony when he was totally deaf.

There's not a high school athletic coach with a decade of experience who can't tell some story of honey in a lion. One such story is now legendary. When Glenn Cunningham was eight years old, he was burned so badly in a schoolhouse fire that his doctor said he would never walk again. But somehow Glenn found the honey of courage and determination in his soul, until he was the prince of American track. I wonder if Cunningham, without his boyhood tragedy, would ever have been more than just an average athlete?

Each time someone polls the American people to learn their favorite hymns, George Bennard's "The Old Rugged Cross" is somewhere in the top half-dozen. Books of hymn stories report only that it was written at a time of trial in Bennard's life; he chose never to discuss the details publicly. But one summer afternoon he told a friend of mine his story. I will respect Bennard's desire for privacy. Let me say only that for him the operative word in the song was "shame." The song came to him at a time when he thought his life and ministry were destroyed. A lion of shame threatened to consume Bennard; instead he found—and gave us—honey.

But it's altogether possible that you don't need my list of examples from history and biography, because you have lived with the lion yourself, and you have found the cache of honey. A good many of us remember some stunning defeat that looked at first like the end of all dreams, but that proved instead to be the beginning of a whole new kind of victory. Others of you remember when sickness threatened everything you cherished; but when it was done, you had found God in a measure you never before thought possible. One day I visited with a man who had just passed through weeks of personal humiliation. "It gave me compassion," he said, "and it carried off a huge store of self-righteousness!"

But don't think I'm simply urging you to be strong in the face of adversity. There's a limit to this business of gritting your teeth, taking hold of your bootstraps, and fighting it out. If I were saying no more than that, I would perhaps be speaking a noble word, but not a truly hopeful one. I want you to know that God is the crucial factor in what I want to leave with you. High resolves and sheer determination are not really enough; they may leave you a hard, unsympathetic person—no winner at all.

As a matter of fact, sometimes our strength gets in the way of our getting the real honey from the lion. The apostle Paul was plagued by something he calls a "thorn in the flesh." Whatever it was (no one will ever on this earth know for sure), he asked God three times that it might be taken from him. Each time, God answered, "My grace is sufficient for you, for power is made perfect in weakness" (2 Corinthians 12:9). Paul concludes that he will "boast all the more gladly" of his weaknesses, because it is through them that the power of Christ is revealed in his life. This may well be the greatest victory of all, to find honey in the lion of our weakness.

I believe that there is *always* honey in the lion. We can always find something to eat in the eater, a sweetness in tragedy. Nature itself seems to dramatize it, as we derive chemicals from ashes, fertilizer from rot and refuse, healing miracles from mold. It is as if God were the ultimate economist, insisting that everything in our universe will eventually—if we will let it—produce good. When we pursue honey in the lion, life is on our side, faith is on our side, *God* is on our side.

But we must go after it. As surely as Samson had to struggle with the lion, reach into the destroyer and get his honey, just so certainly you and I will have to go after the honey of life. It won't force itself on us. If we choose to run from the struggle, or if we allow ourselves to be absorbed with the ghastliness of the slain lion, we will never get the honey that can be ours. Some people are so taken with self-pity that they never get near the potential of beauty. Neither God nor life will make us take the honey. It is there for the person who will say, "I believe that in everything, God works for my good. Therefore I will encounter my sickness, my disappointment, my present defeat, with faith. There is honey in this lion, and I mean someday to have it."

I cannot help being an optimist about life, because I believe in God. I don't ask, nor do I expect, that I should escape from life's issues; I realize that sickness, death, disappointment, and a variety of other problems meet us all, at one time or another. But I am convinced to the core of my being that the lion does not need to be a destroyer. All of life's lions can be a source of honey, if we will make it so.

Don't ask for trouble, of course. Common sense tells us to avoid any pain that isn't necessary, and human compassion tells us to do all we can to save others from suffering. But if trouble comes, and *when* it comes, grasp your lion firmly, and calling—as Samson did—on the Spirit of God, crush defeat in your hands.

Then say to yourself, and say in hope and thanksgiving to God, "Someday I will pass by this place, and I will look again upon this carcass of destruction, this vileness that I wish had never come into my life. And even if it doesn't seem possible now, I know that I will find in the frame of this destroyer a store of honey. There will be something to eat in the eater, and from the strong I will draw something sweet."

That's what I know about life's riddle. By God's help, I will find honey in the lion.

CHAPTER 8

Beauty and the Beast

1 SAMUEL 25:2-42: There was a man in Maon, whose property was in Carmel. The man was very rich; he had three thousand sheep and a thousand goats. He was shearing his sheep in Carmel. Now the name of the man was Nabal, and the name of his wife Abigail. The woman was clever and beautiful, but the man was surly and mean; he was a Calebite. David heard in the wilderness that Nabal was shearing his sheep. So David sent ten young men; and David said to the young men, "Go up to Carmel, and go to Nabal, and greet him in my name. Thus you shall salute him: 'Peace be to you, and peace be to your house, and peace be to all that you have. I hear that you have shearers; now your shepherds have been with us, and we did them no harm, and they missed nothing, all the time they were in Carmel. Ask your young men, and they will tell you. Therefore let my young men find favor in your sight; for we have come on a feast day. Please give whatever you have at hand to your servants and to your son David.' "

When David's young men came, they said all this to Nabal in the name of David; and then they waited. But Nabal answered David's servants, "Who is David? Who is the son of Jesse? There are many servants today who are breaking away from their masters. Shall I take my bread and my water and the meat that I have butchered for my shearers, and give it to men who come from I do not know where?" So David's young men turned away, and came back and told him all this. David said to his men,

"Every man strap on his sword!" And every one of them strapped on his sword; David also strapped on his sword; and about four hundred men went up after David, while two hundred remained with the baggage.

But one of the young men told Abigail, Nabal's wife, "David sent messengers out of the wilderness to salute our master; and he shouted insults at them. Yet the men were very good to us, and we suffered no harm, and we never missed anything when we were in the fields, as long as we were with them; they were a wall to us both by night and by day, all the while we were with them keeping the sheep. Now therefore know this and consider what you should do; for evil has been decided against our master and against all his house; he is so ill-natured that no one can speak to him."

Then Abigail hurried and took two hundred loaves, two skins of wine, five sheep ready dressed, five measures of parched grain, one hundred clusters of raisins, and two hundred cakes of figs. She loaded them on donkeys and said to her young men, "Go on ahead of me; I am coming after you." But she did not tell her husband Nabal. As she rode on the donkey and came down under cover of the mountain, David and his men came down toward her; and she met them. Now David had said, "Surely it was in vain that I protected all that this fellow has in the wilderness, so that nothing was missed of all that belonged to him; but he has returned me evil for good. God do so to David and more also, if by morning I leave so much as one male of all who belong to him."

When Abigail saw David, she hurried and alighted from the donkey, fell before David on her face, bowing to the ground. She fell at his feet and said, "Upon me alone, my lord, be the guilt; please let your servant speak in your ears, and hear the words of your servant. My lord, do not take seriously this ill-natured fellow, Nabal; for as his name is, so is he; Nabal is his name, and folly is with him; but I, your servant, did not see the young men of my lord, whom you sent.

"Now then, my lord, as the LORD lives, and as you yourself live, since the LORD has restrained you from bloodguilt and from taking vengeance with your own hand, now let your enemies and those who seek to do evil to my lord be like Nabal. And now let this present that your servant has brought to my lord be given to the young men who follow my lord. Please forgive the trespass of your servant; for the LORD will certainly make my lord a sure house, because my lord is fighting the battles of the LORD; and evil shall not be found in you so long as you live. If anyone should rise up to pursue you and to seek your life, the life of my lord shall be bound in the bundle of the living under the care of the LORD your God; but the lives of your enemies he shall sling out as from the hollow of a sling. When the LORD has done to my lord according to all the good that he has spoken concerning you, and has appointed you prince over Israel, my lord shall have no cause of grief, or pangs of conscience, for having shed blood without cause or for having saved himself. And when the LORD has dealt well with my lord, then remember your servant."

David said to Abigail, "Blessed be the LORD, the God of Israel, who sent you to meet me today! Blessed be your good sense, and blessed be you, who have kept me today from bloodguilt and from avenging myself by my own hand! For as surely as the LORD the God of Israel lives, who has restrained me from hurting you, unless you had hurried and come to meet me, truly by morning there would not have been left to Nabal so much as one male." Then David received from her hand what she had brought him; he said to her, "Go up to your house in peace; see, I have heeded your voice, and I have granted your petition."

Abigail came to Nabal; he was holding a feast in his house, like the feast of a king. Nabal's heart was merry within him, for he was very drunk; so she told him nothing at all until the morning light. In the morning, when the wine had gone out of Nabal, his wife told him these things, and his heart died within him; he became like a stone. About ten days later the LORD struck Nabal, and he died.

When David heard that Nabal was dead, he said, "Blessed be the LORD who has judged the case of Nabal's insult to me, and has kept back his servant from evil; the LORD has returned the evil-doing of Nabal upon his own head." Then David sent and wooed Abigail, to make her his wife. When David's servants came to Abigail at Carmel, they said to her, "David has sent us to you to take you to him as his wife." She rose and bowed down, with her face to the ground, and said, "Your servant is a slave to wash the feet of the servants of my lord." Abigail got up hurriedly and rode away on a donkey; her five maids attended her. She went after the messengers of David and became his wife.

O ne of my favorite newspaper columnists says that he never goes to see Academy Award movies, because he knows they will always be sad stories; he's looking, he says, for movies with a happy ending. If we are honest, most of us are inclined to favor happy endings. And the more dramatically happy, the better. The more reprehensible the villain or the more hopeless the situation, the greater our satisfaction in seeing a conclusion that says, "and they lived happily ever after."

That's the charm of the French fairy tale "Beauty and the Beast." A beautiful young woman knows that the only way she can save her father's life is to dwell in a palace with a beast. How could a heroine be more truly beautiful, and how could a situation be more utterly hopeless? But she gives herself to the frightening assignment with such kindness and devotion that in time the beast is transformed into a prince. That's a fairy tale, and it ends the way we want it to. And that's the way we want life to be. I suppose that one of the reasons we enjoy fairy tales—whatever our age—is that life doesn't always work out so neatly.

There was a woman long ago named Abigail. She was a beauty; the Bible says so. It also says that she was clever, which probably added to her beauty. She was married to a man named Nabal. He was a beast. The biblical writer describes him as "surly and mean," but I think if you had known him, you would have called him a beast. And all the more so, since he was married to such a wonderful woman. The contrast makes his beastliness all the more obnoxious. You reason that a person who lives with beauty ought in time to be influenced by it. In a sense, that's a point to be inferred from the French fairy tale. And that makes a person feel that Nabal was more of a beast than the one in the fairy tale, because Nabal didn't change. But I'm getting ahead of my story.

In the days when Saul was king of Israel, a young shepherd named David became a national hero. He did it without the help of a public relations firm or a fawning press; it was a matter of extraordinary courage, as well as a populace that was hungry for heroes. Come to think of it, we always are. That's probably why we're so often inclined to manufacture heroes where they don't really exist.

Unfortunately, David's heroism didn't ingratiate him with King Saul. It's very hard for a king to countenance a hero whose public favor is higher than his own, and Saul quite surely couldn't handle it. He became so envious that he resolved to destroy his young competitor. David was forced to flee into exile. But he was such a natural leader that he very quickly gathered about himself a group of fighting men, made up largely of the discredited and disinherited elements of society. They became mercenaries who would fight wherever they were needed, for a price.

I don't think I can compare them to anything in our society. In a very general way, they might be compared to the private security forces which serve businesses and individuals, except that they were not equipped in such a sophisticated fashion. They would protect large landowners from the raiding bands of Bedouin in the area; then they'd ask a fee from the farmer for the services they had rendered. They performed a much-needed service, but not in as tidy a way as modern merchant police would do. The landowners paid only for services truly rendered. Apparently it was an accepted factor in the economy of those times, honorable in its own light, even if quite different from the world we know.

David performed such a service for this man Nabal. With three thousand sheep and a thousand goats, Nabal was one of the wealthier men of his time; he needed protection, and David provided it. Mind you, there was no contract. Such business wasn't conducted that way in those times; terms of remuneration were worked out later.

So David sent ten of his young men to ask payment for the services his men had rendered. Nabal's servants agreed that David's company had performed faithfully. "They were a wall to us," they said, "both by night and by day" (1 Samuel 25:16).

But Nabal treated David's men and their request with exquisite scorn. His reply rings with the arrogance of a man who thinks too well of himself: "Who is David? Who is the son of Jesse? There are many servants today who are breaking away from their masters. Shall I take my bread and my water and the meat that I have butchered for my shearers, and give it to men who come from I do not know where?" (1 Samuel 25:10-11).

When David heard this message, he organized his men for an attack on Nabal. This was what you might call a high-powered collection agency! Those were crude and direct times, where people handled life at its most elemental levels. But meanwhile—fortunately—one of Nabal's servants reported the whole incident to Nabal's wife, the beautiful Abigail. It seems clear that there was a sum of confidence between the servants and Abigail, because they said to her, "Our master is so ill-natured that no one can speak to him." Someone has said that Abigail was as beautiful and sensible as Nabal was churlish and mean. Beauty and beast, indeed! She quickly gathered together a great feast, probably reflecting the adage of another day that the way to a man's heart is through his stomach, and sent it ahead to David, then followed herself.

David had vowed to God that he would kill every man in Nabal's household. But when Abigail appeared, she knelt at his feet and appealed for mercy. "My lord," she said, "do not take seriously this ill-natured fellow, Nabal; for as his name is, so is he; Nabal is his name, and folly is with him" (1 Samuel 25:25).

One wonders about Nabal's name. It meant, literally, *fool.* Did his parents give him such a name? If so, they were surely dooming him, because we tend to live up to the names we're given. Let a youngster be told often enough that he or she is "bright," and the name will come to fit. So, too, with such names as "difficult," "slow," or "spoiled." Or was "Nabal" the name that the man's workers and neighbors gave him, probably never speaking it to him personally but relishing it each time he was the subject of a discussion? I think it may have been the latter.

Abigail reasoned with David. Living with Nabal, she had learned how to deal with men on the edge of violence! Talking with David must have seemed child's play after having to cope with her husband. She insisted that he must not stoop to vengeance, but that he should leave his enemies to the vengeance of

God. She predicted that David would someday be a ruler in Israel, and that when that time came she wanted that he should have "no cause of grief, or pangs of conscience, for having shed blood without cause or for having saved himself " (1 Samuel 25:31). And then she asked that when such power came to him, he would remember her. It was a simple request, but Hollywood would know how to make much of it.

It's easy to see that Abigail was not only charming and beautiful, but that she was also very shrewd. (Perhaps that was Nabal's unwitting gift to her, because one had to be shrewd to survive such a person.) I suspect that shrewdness was a substantial part of her charm; the greatest beauty—and surely the longest-lasting—is always that which springs from inner intelligence and sensitivity. Abigail recognized David's potential. Some people have the gift to see the possibilities in others; they read it the way some investment analysts can anticipate the movement of the stock market. Still more, Abigail saw that David was a basically good human being, and that while at this moment he was operating out of violent anger, he would someday, from a posture of strength, feel ashamed of himself if he allowed these emotions to be expressed.

David was convinced. As much, I'm sure, by her charm as by her good sense and eloquence! And by that I mean no reflection on either Abigail's wisdom or David's methods of reasoning; I'm simply acknowledging that when we human beings make decisions, the elements of the decision-making process are far more complex than we easily recognize. He thanked God that through this woman's intervention he had been kept back from bloodguilt, and from avenging himself, and he assured Abigail that no harm would be done to her household.

When the beauty returned home, she found the beast in full form, in the midst of a drunken celebration. The next morning, "when the wine had gone out of Nabal," she told him all that had happened. The Bible says that "his heart died within him; he became like a stone"; and that ten days later the Lord struck him so that he died (1 Samuel 25:37, 38). Probably a modern pathologist would say that Nabal had an apoplectic seizure. However, modern medical science is coming slowly to recognize the relationship of our emotions to our physical well-being; perhaps someday they will fully grasp what the biblical writer is saying in such an instance as this. If we insist on flouting God's laws—the very laws of the universe—we do, indeed, break ourselves upon them.

When David learned of Nabal's death, he quickly sent a proposal to the beautiful Abigail, asking her to marry him. And that shows that David wasn't so inept, either. Such an early proposal seems highly inappropriate to us, but it was common in the Middle East in those days for a widow to remarry soon after the death of her husband, perhaps because in such a society it was the surest course of economic survival open to a woman.

In its own way, the story of Nabal and Abigail is like a fairy tale, complete with a despicable villain, a beautiful maiden, and an exciting hero. And it ends, as such stories should, with the villain getting his just deserts and the hero and heroine getting each other.

But it's clear that our human stories don't always turn out that way. What shall we say of the beauties who have to go on living in bestial conditions? What of the woman who says, "I kissed a frog, believing he would become a prince, and I've spent the rest of my life living with a frog." The soap opera says that "life can be beautiful," and I happily agree. But life can also be ugly at times, even for beautiful people.

I think of a woman who said to me as a widow, "I lived fifty years with a man who never said a kind word to me, never sympathized with any grief I knew." What then for Beauty and the Beast? I remember a quiet, sensitive man who lived all his adult life with a raucous woman who constantly subjected him to public embarrassment. Now and again one sees an exquisite child growing up in a home of vile harshness. When you observe such instances, you think of flowers that grow in the midst of a city trash heap, and you marvel that such beauty can survive in what is so tawdry and bestial.

I think of those beautiful people whose years are lived out in beastly circumstances. For instance, the persons who carry a physical handicap all their days, a companion tied to them more closely than was Nabal the fool to Abigail the beautiful. Or the person of great sensitivity and talent who lives all her days in circumstances where her talent can never come to fulfillment or even to modest expression. I wonder how many artists died on our nineteenth-century frontier without ever touching a canvas or seeing a painting, or how many composers without ever knowing the song which beat so insistently in their souls? And how many persons just now live and die (usually too soon) in city ghettos without ever putting their beauty on paper, because the beast of their setting won't allow it? Or what shall we say of the person who wants nothing so much as to love and to be loved, yet who lives a lifetime with a beastly loneliness, a thing so real it can almost be touched?

Believe me, many a Beauty lives with a Beast, as surely as Abigail of old was tied to the churlish Nabal. But unlike Abigail, they also die with the beast. What shall we say to such as these?

I think there's as good an answer as can be found in the prayer of the late Reinhold Niebuhr, the premier theologian whose most widely remembered words are paraphrased by millions as the serenity prayer of Alcoholics Anonymous: "God, grant me the serenity to accept the things I cannot change; courage to change the things I can; and wisdom to know the difference."

Some of life's beasts cannot of themselves be changed. Some physical disabilities and limitations, for instance, are beyond the reach of even modern medical science. Such a person must then stop beating uselessly against the wall and rise up to live with serenity, composure, and victory. But some things—indeed, most things—can be changed, and if that be so, we must take hold of life with courage and change what we can. And with it all, we must seek the wisdom to know what can be changed and what cannot, then live accordingly.

Life (or more correctly, death) interceded for Abigail. Most of us, however, have to deal with our circumstances and situations as we find them. It's our business to find as much beauty as we can, and by the grace of God, deal intelligently, directly, and victoriously with that which is beastly. And with it all to know, as the wise and beautiful Abigail put it, that our lives "shall be bound in the bundle of the living under the care of the LORD [our] God" (1 Samuel 25:29).

CHAPTER 9

A Refugee
at the King's Table

2 SAMUEL 9:1-13: David asked, "Is there still anyone left of the house of Saul to whom I may show kindness for Jonathan's sake?" Now there was a servant of the house of Saul whose name was Ziba, and he was summoned to David. The king said to him, "Are you Ziba?" And he said, "At your service!" The king said, "Is there anyone remaining of the house of Saul to whom I may show the kindness of God?" Ziba said to the king, "There remains a son of Jonathan; he is crippled in his feet." The king said to him, "Where is he?" Ziba said to the king, "He is in the house of Machir son of Ammiel, at Lodebar." Then King David sent and brought him from the house of Machir son of Ammiel, at Lodebar. Mephibosheth son of Jonathan son of Saul came to David, and fell on his face and did obeisance. David said, "Mephibosheth!" He answered, "I am your servant." David said to him, "Do not be afraid, for I will show you kindness for the sake of your father Jonathan; I will restore to you all the land of your grandfather Saul, and you yourself shall eat at my table always." He did obeisance and said, "What is your servant, that you should look upon a dead dog such as I?"

Then the king summoned Saul's servant Ziba, and said to him, "All that belonged to Saul and to all his house I have given to your master's grandson. You and your sons and your servants shall till the land for him, and shall bring in the produce, so that your master's grandson may have food to eat; but your master's grandson Mephibosheth shall always eat at my table." Now Ziba had fifteen sons and twenty servants. Then Ziba said to the king, "According to all that my lord the king commands his servant, so your servant will do." Mephibosheth ate at David's table, like one of the king's sons. Mephibosheth had a young son whose name was Mica. And all who lived in Ziba's house became Mephibosheth's servants. Mephibosheth lived in Jerusalem, for he always ate at the king's table. Now he was lame in both his feet.

Sometimes when I receive holy communion, I look at myself and think I see a man named Mephibosheth. A strange name of which to be reminded? The man's story is still more strange. But at the communion table I see myself in him. I look in the mirror of the sacrament, and the face looking back at me is the face of Mephibosheth. And the frame of the picture is called grace.

Let me tell you his story, because I confess that it is not a familiar one—not unless you're a fairly enthusiastic student of the Hebrew Scriptures. Mephibosheth came from a remarkable family; at the time of his birth, his future seemed assured and exceedingly bright. His grandfather, Saul, was the first king of the nation of Israel, and was on the throne at the time Mephibosheth was born. Saul was a handsome, powerful man (the biblical writer says that he "stood head and shoulders above everyone else" [1 Samuel 9:2]). At the beginning of his reign, he was an effective leader and a great general. The boy's father was Jonathan, who was next in line for the throne, and a great leader in his own right. In fact, if Jonathan had lived and had become king, he would probably have been a better king than was his father. Jonathan was not only a sterling leader, he was also a very good human being who, besides all his strength, possessed character and gentleness.

So Mephibosheth was born to privilege, position, and power. I venture that the royal court and the whole nation fawned on his infancy. What he did must have been a topic of excited street-corner gossip. When most children learn to walk or begin to talk, the achievement delights parents and grandparents and a few enlisted friends of the family; when this child took his first steps, half a nation smiled in proud pleasure.

Then suddenly, violently, everything was changed. His father and grandfather went off to battle to defend their nation against their traditional enemy, the Philistines. The Israelites were defeated badly; indeed, they were routed in battle. And in the process, both the father and the grandfather of Mephibosheth, King Saul and Prince Jonathan, were killed. The royal palace, which until then had been a haven of safety and luxury, was now the most dangerous place in the country , since it was the power center of the nation.

In the terror and confusion of retreat, a faithful royal nurse grabbed young Mephibosheth and fled. The boy was only five years old at the time. As they ran from the palace, the little boy fell and was severely injured. Perhaps if he could have received early, careful medical attention, the injury wouldn't have been so threatening, but under the circumstances of flight, the nurse couldn't seek out any professional assistance. As a result, the boy became permanently lame in both his feet, crippled for life.

So it was that overnight the boy who had been a prince became an exile, and a child who had possessed the natural ability to leap and run became physically limited. Meanwhile, the brilliant warrior, David, established himself on the throne of Israel; he not only restored the nation to its former glory, but he brought it to a prominence in the company of nations which it had never previously known.

Then one day King David made an inquiry: "Is there still anyone left of the house of Saul to whom I may show kindness for Jonathan's sake?" (2 Samuel 9:1). David and Jonathan had been the closest of friends during Jonathan's lifetime, so now David hoped he could pay tribute to that friendship by a kindness to some lost descendant. He learned that Mephibosheth, son of Jonathan, was still alive, and in hiding. When the young man was brought to David, he came fearfully, probably thinking the King would now destroy him. Instead David said, "Do not be afraid, for I will show you kindness for the sake of your father Jonathan;

I will restore to you all the land of your grandfather Saul, and you yourself shall eat at my table always" (2 Samuel 9:7).

So the young man moved from exile back into the property of his family. He was provided with servants. And the scripture says, "Mephibosheth lived in Jerusalem, for he always ate at the king's table. Now he was lame in both his feet" (2 Samuel 9:13).

The story doesn't end there. There's another chapter, and it's a somewhat perplexing one. Nearly twenty years later one of David's own sons, Absalom, organized a revolt against the king, and for several days David had to flee from his palace. Those who were loyal fled with him, while some remained behind and cast their lot with Absalom. Mephibosheth's servant joined David, bringing a great store of food with him, but when David asked about Mephibosheth, the servant said that he had stayed behind in Jerusalem in the hope that he might now gain the throne which had once been his grandfather's.

The story seemed plausible, and David believed it. He promised that when he was returned to power he would see to it that the servant received the property which had once belonged to Mephibosheth. But when David returned to Jerusalem, Mephibosheth came to meet him. The scripture says that he had not dressed his feet nor trimmed his beard nor washed his clothes from the day David left until he returned in peace. He insisted that, contrary to the servant's report, he had been left without a way to escape. He defended his loyalty to David. After all, he said, all of his father's house were but dead men before the king—that is, the king held over them absolute power of life and death. And yet the king had chosen instead to deliver Mephibosheth from exile and to give him a place at the king's own table. David felt he was caught between conflicting reports which left him with no way of discerning the truth, so he decreed that Mephibosheth's property should be divided between Mephibosheth and his servant.

Mephibosheth's story is a kind of parable to me—perhaps even a short allegory—and its climax comes at the table of communion. Mephibosheth was born well—the child of a king. And so were we all. When we human creatures came to birth, the morning stars sang together and the whole creation rejoiced in such a climax to God's grand work of creation. If some voice in the symphony of the ages had asked, "Whom do these human creatures resemble?" eternity would have answered, "They are only a little lower than God, crowned with glory and honor" (Psalm 8:5); and still another voice might have added, "It's clear enough: they are made in the image of God, and the breath of God is in them" (Genesis 1:27; 2:7). We started well, no doubt about it! How better can you start than to be in God's own image?

But somewhere along the way, like Mephibosheth, we suffered a fall. This fall of ours is a strange story. Several years ago a graduate student who was seeking opinions to include in his dissertation asked me if I believed in original sin. "Not in theory," I said, "only in fact." That is, I don't believe that every person is born condemned because of the sin of Adam; but I observe, in the run of daily living, that every person is born "with a pack on his back." All of us find ourselves burdened with the inheritance of human conduct; yes, one might even say, of human tendency and inclination. Deep grooves seem to be graven into our human psyche so that we often fall below our own best intentions.

Medical people sometimes tell us that the best way to avoid heart attacks is to choose the right ancestors. Ours is a mixed story. We started well, but these ancient ancestors, whom we call Adam and Eve, went off the track, and our human race has been sickly ever since. We sometimes put the matter in practical, personal terms. "I have my father's moodiness," we say; or, "I'm afraid I inherited my Aunt Tillie's tongue." When we speak that way, we confess that the blood of Adam and Eve flows in our veins and that we are constantly struggling to rise above the heritage of our fallen state.

Now of course Mephibosheth wasn't entirely responsible for his disability. The accident happened when he was so young as to be hardly able to prevent it. He was, as we say, a victim of circumstances. And aren't we all? If I think long enough about anyone's sins, I find myself being sorry for him or her. I think of her neighborhood, her bad companions, the failure of some teacher or minister or parent, a poor heredity—and I'm ready to say, "The poor soul was crippled by life before she really had a chance." Like Mephibosheth. If there is any measurable logic in what we call amazing grace, it probably lies right here, that our condition was not all our own fault; we are products of a long line of trouble!

But we must also say that—like Mephibosheth—what we do with our condition is our own responsibility. We may be part of a fallen race, but our response to this condition can be that of a Francis of Assisi or of an Attila the Hun. We choose the continuing direction.

At any rate, we live in exile. The preacher tells us we're made in the image of God, but we don't feel like it. Then one day we hear the Good News. For Mephibosheth it came in David's question, "Is there anyone left of the house of Saul, that I may show him kindness for Jonathan's sake?" Mephibosheth was called by the king, not on the basis of any personal merit, but because the king was generous and because he wanted to honor another. We sing a hymn which celebrates such divine generosity:

> Amazing grace, how sweet the sound,
> That saved a wretch like me;
> I once was lost, but now am found,
> Was blind, but now I see.

Mephibosheth was not only lost, he was also in hiding. The same might be said of us. We seem at times to be in flight from God. But "amazing grace" pursues us until at last we respond.

When Mephibosheth came into the palace on King David's invitation, he stumbled in on crippled feet. Biblical accounts are almost always succinct and spare in their language, but this brief story chooses to repeat the description of the young man's condition, giving it emphasis out of proportion to what seems its importance. When King David asks if any descendant of Saul still lives, the servant replies, "There remains a son of Jonathan; he is crippled in his feet" (2 Samuel 9:3). He might so easily have mentioned his age as a first factor of interest, or something about his family circumstances, but instead—"he is crippled in his feet." And when the primary unit of the story ends, it is with the sentence, "Now he was lame in both his feet" (2 Samuel 9:13).

In biblical times, great store was laid on physical powers, even in the qualifications for the priesthood; and perhaps above all, a man might be judged by his legs. His hands represented skill, but the measure of manliness was in the legs, for theirs was a world where fleetness of foot so often determined success in battle and very survival. In the same way the feet and legs carried a kind of spiritual symbolism. When the prophet Habakkuk testified to God's help through the trials of life, he said that God had made his feet like those of a mountain deer, so that he was able to tread safely on life's high and perilous places (Habakkuk 3:19).

I come to God as Mephibosheth came to King David. When the prodigal returns home, he is not usually a pretty sight. Noble, yes, because he is forsaking sin and coming home; but not pretty. Some are offended that they must approach God by the route of repentance. The ancient communion ritual has us say, "We do earnestly repent and are heartily sorry for these our mis-doings. . . ." How else would one come to the King of the Universe, except by way of repentance?

I said at the outset that often, at the communion table, I look at myself and see the man named Mephibosheth. I'm thinking especially of this verse: "For he always ate at the king's table. Now he was lame in both his feet" (2 Samuel 9:13). Four times in this short account we are told that he ate at the king's table; this is a recurring theme along with the description of his physical brokenness. He had been in exile, but now he had been accepted into the king's family: He ate at the royal table.

And at this table, his helplessness is hidden. His disability does not frustrate him here; in this place, the tragedy of his past is out of sight. Here, all that is seen of him is able and adequate.

And so it is with me—and with you—when we come to the table of our Lord. The tragedy of our human sinfulness is covered at this table. Here our transgressions are forgiven, never to be remembered against us any more. We eat like sons and daughters of the king, the long years of our exile forgotten.

But we remember that after perhaps twenty years of eating at the king's table, a shadow comes across Mephibosheth's life. At the time of Absalom's rebellion against David, it was said that Mephibosheth was a traitor; and while the biblical writer seems to offer some defense for the man, the case is never fully settled. Whether or not he failed, we only know that King David accepted him back into his household.

Most of us understand this part of the story, at least from a personal point of view. Even though we have been accepted at the King's table, we have sometimes been in-and-out, up-and-down, vacillating and undependable. A critic might question our loyalty and our deserving. We haven't always, unfailingly, stood with the King, even though we have been blessed by divine kindliness.

But God's grace is greater than our sins, and greater too than our inconsistencies. It is steadfast enough to overcome our vacillations. So again we come to our Lord's table: hobbled, perhaps, and not as pretty as we would like. But at this magnificent board, our helplessness is hidden. We have been taken into the family of God. We dare to eat at the table of the King.

In Defense of Job's Wife

JOB 2:1-10: One day the heavenly beings came to present themselves before the LORD, and Satan also came among them to present himself before the LORD. The LORD said to Satan, "Where have you come from?" Satan answered the LORD, "From going to and fro on the earth, and from walking up and down on it." The LORD said to Satan, "Have you considered my servant Job? There is no one like him on the earth, a blameless and upright man who fears God and turns away from evil. He still persists in his integrity, although you incited me against him, to destroy him for no reason." Then Satan answered the LORD, "Skin for skin! All that people have they will give to save their lives.

But stretch out your hand now and touch his bone and his flesh, and he will curse you to your face." The LORD said to Satan, "Very well, he is in your power; only spare his life."

So Satan went out from the presence of the LORD, and inflicted loathsome sores on Job from the sole of his foot to the crown of his head. Job took a potsherd with which to scrape himself, and sat among the ashes.

Then his wife said to him, "Do you still persist in your integrity? Curse God, and die." But he said to her, "You speak as any foolish woman would speak. Shall we receive the good at the hand of God, and not receive the bad?" In all this Job did not sin with his lips.

*I*t's time someone said a good word for Job's wife. Over the centuries she has suffered more than her share of being maligned. She hasn't become quite as infamous as Job's friends, but of course she shouldn't be. Those dubious friends spent many thousands of words making Job miserable, while Job's wife is credited with only two brief sentences—a rhetorical question and its answer. In most of our English translations, the two sentences add up to fewer than a dozen words.

Let me confess that it may be guilt that makes me so anxious to raise a case for this woman, because I, too, have several times treated her with disrespect. I've been known to refer to her with the kind of humor we men sometimes use when talking about women, wives, and marriage. So I'm anxious to tell you her side of the story, as I see it. It's partly an act of penance for me. I apologize, too, for speaking of her only as "Job's wife"; I'm sorry for this demeaning anonymity. But it's something I can't help, because for some reason the biblical writer never tells us her name. And before you charge the original author with male chauvinism, let me note that when Job's fortunes are restored, at the end of the story, and he once again has seven sons and three daughters, it is only the daughters who are identified by name. Even then, however, Job's wife remains anonymous.

Job was a man of enormous wealth. The biblical writer says that he was "the greatest of all the people of the east" (Job 1:3). Job and his wife had every advantage wealth could offer in their day; and while that didn't include such modern advantages as computers, televisions, and videocassette recorders, it did mean a full retinue of servants and probably a different menu every day of the week, one that any modern person might envy. They had a lovely family, too, with seven sons and three daughters. It was a family where the siblings got along so well that the sons would hold feasts in one another's houses in turn, and would invite their sisters to join them.

And with it all, Job was a good man. The writer says that he was "blameless and upright," fearing God and scrupulously avoiding evil. He was so sensitive to the possibility of evil, in fact, that whenever his sons would have one of their feasts, he would rise early in the morning to offer burnt sacrifices on their behalf, just in case they might have done wrong. His wealth, privilege, and success seemed not to have spoiled him at all.

All of which is to say that Job's wife was enjoying a very comfortable way of life; not only was she wealthy, she had a beautiful family and a husband who must have made her the envy of many of her neighbors. A modern observer might note that a woman who has borne ten children has had her share of pain, and I readily concur. But this, too, needs to be seen in the context of its time, because in that ancient world a large family was seen as evidence of divine blessing. Yes, Job's wife had a good life.

But then disaster struck. Not once, but again and again, as if Job were the devil's favorite target—as indeed, he was!—and not over a long period of time, so there would be opportunity to recover, but in a swift succession of blows. All of the vast family wealth was wiped out in a series of dramatic misfortunes. Then the seven sons and three daughters were killed when a desert storm blew down the house in which they were celebrating together, in one of their traditional banquets. This time Job didn't have opportunity to plead their case with a morning sacrifice.

Soon thereafter, Job himself suffered a devastating illness. We're told that the adversary asked especially for the chance to attack Job's body. Modern medical science would probably say that no such additional authorization was needed; psychosomatically, anyone who had gone through such a series of personal disasters was a natural candidate for illness—particularly the kind of illness that came to Job. We're never given a clear medical description of his affliction; we're told only that he had "loathsome sores . . . from the sole of his foot to the crown of his head" (Job 2:7).

He must have been a pathetic sight; yes, a repulsive one. He chose to go out to a garbage heap and there to scrape away at the discharge of his body, using a piece of broken pottery. One has the feeling that this was virtually all he had left. Or was it perhaps that he found himself so distasteful that there was a kind of perverse pleasure in treating his wounds with an implement of brokenness?

At that point Job's wife enters the story. Until now, she hasn't been mentioned; and as it happens, she will not be mentioned again. For only this brief moment, she steps on stage, in order to deliver her soul. "Do you still persist in your integrity?" she asks. And then she answers for herself, perhaps because she knows Job will contradict her. "Curse God, and die" (Job 2:9).

The speech is short and to the point. She doesn't rant or rave, nor does she lay blame. There is a hint of impatience with Job's piety—the impatience one may feel when dealing with a quality of life that seems incomprehensible. Job's answer is equally brief. At worst, it sounds like bitter anger, and at best, like righteous indignation: "You speak as any foolish woman would speak. Shall we receive the good at the hand of God, and not receive the bad?" (Job 2:10).

Now without a doubt, Job's wife doesn't look very good in this conversation. She seems to have given up on God and life and integrity. "Curse God and die," she says. I acknowledge that her response isn't as inspiring as Job's, nor is it marked by such heroic faith. We want her to embrace Job's poor, ulcerated body and say, "We'll see this through together. God helping us, we'll see it through."

But I wonder if perhaps she was responding the way many a sympathetic, compassionate spouse might respond? Was she saying, "Dear Job, you've suffered long enough. No one can expect you to take any more, not even God. You have a right to die." If that's what she meant, I will still concede that she was making a slightly lower response of faith. But if I'm right in thinking that perhaps she was trying in her own way to help her husband, and if it was true that she was moved by compassion, even if in a temper of hopelessness—well, let us give her credit for that. Her actions may not have been a model of faith, but I admire her human loyalty.

And let's go a step farther. Everybody talks about how much Job endured in his loss of wealth and in the deaths of his children. But remember that Job's wife suffered the same losses. As a matter of fact, it can well be argued that her sense of loss in the death of her children was even greater than Job's. I remember a fine preacher-scholar who recalled the pain he and his wife suffered in the death, almost immediately after birth, of their first child. "She suffered more than I," he said, "because she suffered bodily as well as emotionally. I only went through it emotionally." There's probably no adequate way to compare a mother's and a father's sense of loss, because our genes and personalities are different. But no matter; at the least, Job's wife must have been as bereft by the death of her children as was Job. And she was just as inconvenienced by his financial reverses, too. If Job had nothing left but a garbage heap, that's all she had, as well. So all of this pain that descended on Job descended with equal force on Job's wife.

But wait, someone says; Job had the additional suffering of his bodily affliction. True. But even here I want to say a word for Job's wife, one that reflects my thirty-eight years as a parish pastor. During those years I so often studied the special, back-of-the-scenes pain of the people who stand alongside the sufferers. And I have concluded that at times, in certain immeasurable ways, the dear friend, spouse, or parent of a sufferer may go through something almost as bad as what the sufferer is experiencing. Indeed, in its own peculiar way—a way that it is impossible to measure—the suffering of the person standing alongside may at times be worse.

I'm speaking of the element of hopelessness and helplessness. How often I've heard a family member say, while watching at a hospital bed or at the chair of invalidism, "If only there were something I could do—something *real*—to take some of the pain." C. S. Lewis felt this so deeply during the illness of his wife, Joy, that—influenced by the teachings of his friend, Charles Williams—he literally absorbed some of Joy's pain, to her relief. He found gladness in doing so. But not many people have such an extraordinary experience. More often they feel, after doing everything in their power, that they haven't done enough. And sometimes, unfortunately, the person suffering even lets them know that it isn't enough! In any event, the person standing alongside has to cope with a desperately helpless feeling.

So when I say a good word for Job's wife, I'm trying to say a word of sympathy for those persons who watch at the bedside of the terminally ill—particularly those instances where the ill person suffers for months or even years. I think of all those parents who have watched with ill children, all those spouses who have stayed near a bedside, all those adult children who have presided over a lengthy illness for a parent. As all such persons know, it isn't easy to be Job's wife.

And with the danger of going from the sublime to the mundane, let me take the matter another step farther. I'm thinking of all those secretaries and executive assistants who work for difficult bosses, or for bosses who have especially difficult jobs. It's true that the buck stops with the executive, but it's also true that he or she is paid more bucks for doing the job. And it's equally true that in many instances the executive wouldn't be able to do his or her job if it weren't for some faithful, often unheralded assistant or secretary.

Sometimes when the going gets tough, the assistant suffers almost as much as the boss, not only because their fortunes are so closely tied, but also because of the loyalty of the assistant. I think I've seen instances where the assistant suffered even more, because of a high level of conscientiousness and feelings of responsibility. Not always, of course; I've known assistants who went home early and worried little; they reasoned that they weren't paid to worry! But there are some who, like Job's wife, are on the near edge of all the pain, and get little praise for it. At best, they get a gracious nod at the executive's farewell banquet; "I never could have done it," the boss says expansively (and probably very earnestly), "if it hadn't been for the people working with me." Perhaps they will even be named.

Sometimes Job's wife is a husband. I knew a man whose wife was a powerful, dramatic personality. She was an effective preacher and leader many years before women began to enter the ministry in greater numbers. He was a quiet, standby sort of man, with a self-deprecating sense of humor. "I'm the joker in the king's deck," he would always say by way of self-introduction—often in situations where he had almost been missed while attention was paid to his spouse. But he was so wonderfully proud! "Jeannette is a remarkable woman," he would say. Some people saw him as a buffoon; others thought he was a bit odd. He didn't fit the conventional role of a male in the world of the 1940s. But he gladly put his pride and personal ambition aside to further the work of another.

Who can say what sacrifices some spouses have paid for their companion's work? Often it means moving when they would rather stay put, or going to social engagements where they feel uncomfortable, or listening to conversations that are tedious for an outsider. And so very often it means being the lightning rod for the other person's worries and tensions. He or she restrains emotions all through a difficult day in business or profession, then lets them out at home, making spouse—and perhaps children, too—the victim of anger which ought to have been directed elsewhere. In my mind, such persons belong to the honorable order of Job's wife.

At a ceremony at Arlington, some years ago, the President honored a young Army sergeant, the father of three children, with a posthumous Medal of Honor. In a rice paddy in Vietnam he had thrown himself on a live mine, taking the full blast into his body, in order to save the lives of his fellow soldiers. When the President gave the Medal to the young widow, he said, as he saw her holding back her tears, "You're a brave young woman." She replied, "Mr. President, I have to be brave because he was brave."

Call her Job's wife. And honor the fact that while her husband's almost monumental bravery represented a split second of decision and terror, hers calls for a hundred lonely nights with sick children, attending dozens of PTA meetings alone, and trying to be both mother and father at all of those soccer games and parties. It isn't easy to be Job's wife, to stand alongside a hero.

Long, long ago the great King David had a word for this. When his army was in battle, there came an occasion when some of the soldiers couldn't continue on, so they were left to guard the supplies. In time the fighting army returned victorious, with the usual spoils of war. David proceeded to distribute the spoils equally among all the soldiers. Some objected, because they felt that those who had guarded the supplies didn't deserve an equal share with those who went into the battle. But King David answered, "The share of the one who goes down into the battle shall be the same as the share of the one who stays by the baggage" (1 Samuel 30:24).

John Milton got the message another way in his personal experience of blindness. He felt that he was useless now that his sight was gone, and that his one great gift of eloquence would lie wasted. But then it seemed to Milton that God answered:

> God does not need
> Either man's work or his own gifts. Who best
> Bear his mild yoke, they serve him best. His state
> Is kingly; thousands at his bidding speed,
> And post o'er land and ocean without rest;
> They also serve who only stand and wait.

Some people, in the nature of life and its transient assignments, are called at times to "stand and wait." They have the role of Job's wife. It isn't an easy one. I like to believe that God sees and understands, and that in the final judgment, when all the issues of life are made clear, God will see that proper credit is paid.

CHAPTER 11

Jonah's Christmas Story

JONAH 3:1-6, 10: The word of the LORD came to Jonah a second time, saying, "Get up, go to Nineveh, that great city, and proclaim to it the message that I tell you." So Jonah set out and went to Nineveh, according to the word of the LORD. Now Nineveh was an exceedingly large city, a three days' walk across. Jonah began to go into the city, going a day's walk. And he cried out, "Forty days more, and Nineveh shall be overthrown!" And the people of Nineveh believed God; they proclaimed a fast, and everyone, great and small, put on sackcloth.

When the news reached the king of Nineveh, he rose from his throne, removed his robe, covered himself with sackcloth, and sat in ashes. . . .

When God saw what they did, how they turned from their evil ways, God changed his mind about the calamity that he had said he would bring upon them; and he did not do it.

MATTHEW 12:38-42: Then some of the scribes and Pharisees said to him, "Teacher, we wish to see a sign from you." But he answered them, "An evil and adulterous generation asks for a sign, but no sign will be given to it except the sign of the prophet Jonah. For just as Jonah was three days and three nights in the belly of the sea monster, so for three days and three nights the Son of Man will be in the heart of the earth. The people of Nineveh will rise up at the judgment with this generation and condemn it, because they repented at the proclamation of Jonah, and see, something greater than Jonah is here! The queen of the South will rise up at the judgment with this generation and condemn it, because she came from the ends of the earth to listen to the wisdom of Solomon, and see, something greater than Solomon is here!

*Q*uickly, now: If you're asked to think of a Christmas villain, who comes to mind? Those who read Dr. Seuss to their children or those who as children heard Dr. Seuss may answer, "the Grinch that stole Christmas." But every generation for the past 125 years will say, even more emphatically, "*Scrooge.*" His name is so synonymous with a certain kind of holiday malevolence that it has gone into our dictionaries. Many of us can quote, in some fashion, Charles Dickens' description: "Oh! But he was a tight-fisted hand at the grindstone, was Scrooge! a squeezing, wrenching, grasping, scraping, clutching, covetous old sinner!" Scrooge is the diametrical opposite of the Christmas spirit.

But Charles Dickens didn't invent Scrooge, he simply gave him a name. As a matter of fact, Scrooge is a bit of a novice at missing the Christmas spirit. When Dickens unfolds Scrooge's story, in Christmas Past, we can understand how he went wrong. I can't make such a case for the original Scrooge. What's more, Dickens' Scrooge was converted—magnificently, so that there was no man in all of London town who celebrated Christmas better. But as far as we know, the ancient Scrooge who is on my mind may not have been converted. His conclusion is left unsettled.

I'm speaking of a man named Jonah, a prophet of the Lord God. And before you write me off by muttering, "Jonah's a fish story, not a Christmas story," I ask you to hear me out. When I'm done, perhaps you'll agree that Jonah is a Christmas story in its own right, and that Jonah himself was the original, archetypal Scrooge.

As a prophet of God, it was Jonah's business to deliver the counsel of God wherever it might be needed. But when God told him to go to Nineveh to preach, he immediately set sail in the opposite direction. He chose Tarshish, the farthest reach of the ancient world. And the book that tells his story leaves no question as to why he was making the trip; he was seeking "to flee . . . from the presence of the LORD" (Jonah 1:3).

As soon as he boarded the ship, Jonah went below deck to sleep. But very shortly the sailors awakened him. The ship was about to be wiped out in a storm, and the sailors were suspicious of a man who could sleep through a storm of such intensity. He confessed that he was no doubt the cause of their trouble, and he urged that they throw him overboard so that the ship might be saved.

The sailors were reluctant, but, operating on the ancient principle "Better you than us," they finally threw him into the sea. Jonah was immediately swallowed by a great fish. Inside the fish, he began to pray, pleading with God to hear him and to save him. At God's command, Jonah was vomited onto dry land, and there, once again, the Lord commissioned him to go to Nineveh.

This time he went (I'm not surprised!). And although he preached rather unwillingly, his efforts were effective. So effective, in fact, that the whole city—a notoriously wicked place—repented. Even the king put on the garments of repentance in an act of public submission. As a result, Nineveh was spared from the judgment which Jonah had prophesied.

Now that should have made Jonah happy. How could a preacher ask for greater success? Instead, however, he became so angry that he prayed he might die. God asked, "Do you have a right to be this angry?"—and Jonah answered, "I certainly do. I'm angry enough to die." But the Lord said, "You worry about a vine that grows one day and dies the next. Shouldn't I care about a city of 120,000 people who are ignorant and lost?" And with that question—but with no answer from Jonah—the book ends.

Now that's a Christmas story. It is probably the strongest—and surely the most dramatic—statement anywhere in the Hebrew Scriptures that God loves everyone, and that he doesn't want anyone to perish. The New Testament sums up the Christmas story in a single verse: "For God so loved the world that he gave his only Son, so that everyone who believes in him may not perish but may have eternal life" (John 3:16). The story in the book of Jonah gets at the same idea by identifying the nation most difficult to love and saying, in effect, "God so loved Nineveh that he sent Jonah to preach to them."

But Jonah was a Scrooge. He didn't want to see the people of Nineveh saved. God wanted to celebrate Christmas in Nineveh, so to speak, to tell that wicked, brutal city that he loved them, but Jonah didn't have the Christmas spirit. God said, "Isn't it wonderful that the people of Nineveh want to be saved?"—and Jonah answered, "Bah! Humbug!"

Now mind you, Jonah had his reasons. The people of Nineveh weren't very nice folks. They were ruthless in battle and vicious in conquest. They weren't satisfied to defeat their enemies; instead, they seemed to delight in torturing and humiliating them. History reports that when their armies marched into cities and villages, their soldiers would with their swords tear open women who were great with child. Jonah believed that God was just, and that therefore the Ninevites would eventually get what they deserved. So when God asked him to call the people of Nineveh to repent, Jonah simply couldn't do it. He didn't want them to repent; he wanted them to suffer the way they'd made others suffer. He feared that if he preached to them, his preaching would succeed and they would change their ways, in which event God might withhold the judgment they had coming to them. And as it worked out, his worst fears about the goodness of God proved true.

So Jonah couldn't sing, "Joy to the world, the Lord is come!" He was willing to sing, "Joy to my people"; he might even have gone so far as to sing, "Joy to everyone but the Ninevites." But he couldn't possibly sing "Joy to the world," because he didn't want the whole world to find joy. He hoped that God's joy would be selective, coming only to those persons who appealed to God— and yes, to those who, by his judgment, deserved joy.

And here, dear friends, is the quality of Christmas. It has been given to us not because we deserve it, but because we need it. God gave us Christmas, not on the basis of our merits, but on account of God's own love. *Grace,* we call it; and Christmas is the very essence of grace.

So the story of Jonah tells us, hundreds of years before the first Christmas, that Christmas was on the way. Jonah learned that God cares not only for the attractive people, the chosen people, and the deserving people, but also for the people who, by all logic, deserve to be despised. As you read Jonah's story, you sense that there is a loving rumbling going on in heaven, and you know that someday, something wonderful is going to happen—just as it did, a few centuries later, in Bethlehem.

But see the proportions of the Christmas story. Jonah was called to preach to his enemies; Jesus was asked to *die* for them. Jonah was unwilling to go until he was forced to do so; Jesus said, "My food is to do the will of him who sent me" (John 4:34). Jonah spent three days in the belly of a great fish because he was running from God. Jesus spent three days in the belly of the earth because he was running *for* God. Jonah went into the prison of a fish because he was disobedient; Jesus went into the prison of earth and death as an act of obedient love.

Jonah's Christmas story is a lovely foreshadowing of what was to come. It shows us what God had in mind. It also shows us how difficult it may be for some of us humans to catch God's Christmas spirit.

What God has in mind is love for the whole human race, and through that love, salvation. Let us be very clear about this: Christmas is not only more than parties and festivities, it is more even than our usual kind of giving. When we speak of "the Christmas spirit," we're generally working on too small a definition. The ultimate act of Christmas is that God loved our world so profoundly that he gave his only Son for our salvation. Jonah may have rejected the Christmas spirit, but at least he knew what he was rejecting. You and I are more likely to be quietly misled into a variation on Christmas which misses the real thing.

I don't mean to take the lovely, sentimental elements from you; the truth is, I love them, too. But I want us to have the real thing. I love to think about "chestnuts roasting on an open fire," even though I've never seen it happen, and I'm as ready as anyone to sing, "I'm dreaming of a white Christmas." But I need to remember that these are secondary and derivative, and that if I lose what is primary, all of the secondary is not only meaningless, it will eventually cease to exist. I want to give presents, and I guess I enjoy receiving them, too. I'm all for sending and getting greeting cards. But with all of that, I want to remember that the point of Christmas is not cards and it is not even giving; it is that God so loved the world that he chose to send his Son, via a peasant girl from Nazareth. It is that God loves even Nineveh.

Believe me, that's the best news I can report, at Christmas or at any other time. On the surface, you and I are not as bad as the people of ancient Nineveh. We can't even imagine ourselves involved in deeds like theirs. Yet we are infected with the same basic disease of sin, and while we are more civilized, we are still—now and then—pretty unlovable ourselves. We need a Savior.

And the worst moments come when we feel that we're unlovable. I think of a college student who came to my study years ago for counsel. "I just hate myself," she said. "I like you," I answered; and she quickly replied, "But you don't know me the way I do." And that's the way each of us sometimes feels about himself or herself. We feel like Nineveh. So we wouldn't be terribly surprised if we heard that some new Jonah would rather be shipwrecked and swallowed by a fish than have to embrace us. How magnificent, at such a time, to hear about Christmas! God so loved us—any and all of us!—that he came to Bethlehem and eventually to Calvary and to three days in the belly of death, in order to bring us to himself. That's better than chestnuts on an open fire, a red-nosed reindeer, and mommy kissing Santa Claus!

As I said earlier, the story of Jonah ends with a question mark. Jonah is angry, and God is reasoning with him, trying to persuade him to have a little heart for the people of Nineveh. But we're never told how Jonah responded. Of course that's the whole point of the book. The Hebrews of that long-ago time were supposed to answer the question for themselves. And we, today, are called upon to do the same.

So here's the Christmas question for you and me: If God so loved the world that he would send his Son to save the people of Nineveh, New York, Las Vegas, Tokyo, and Baghdad, and all points north, south, east, and west, what kind of love ought we then to show, if we claim to have experienced God's love?

That is: If God would ask us to pray for the Ninevites in our own lives—the persons who have hurt us, lied about us, and made us miserable, or the groups of people we find it hard to look upon kindly—if God would ask us to pray for them, give to their needs, or extend an arm of mercy and embrace to them, how would we respond? Would we, like Jonah, choose rather to flee to the farthest reaches of Tarshish?

I hope not. Since we have received the grace of God, I hope we will be ready to share it. Maybe we can learn from Jonah and his later descendant, Scrooge, and live in the spirit of the One who gave us Christmas.

CHAPTER *12*

God Is Better Than His Plans

RUTH 1:1-5; 4:13-17: In the days when the judges ruled, there was a famine in the land, and a certain man of Bethlehem in Judah went to live in the country of Moab, he and his wife and two sons. The name of the man was Elimelech and the name of his wife Naomi, and the names of his two sons were Mahlon and Chilion; they were Ephrathites from Bethlehem in Judah. They went into the country of Moab and remained there. But Elimelech, the husband of Naomi, died, and she was left with her two sons. These took Moabite wives; the name of the one was Orpah and the name of the other Ruth. When they had lived there about ten years, both Mahlon and Chilion also died, so that the woman was left without her two sons and her husband. . . .

So Boaz took Ruth and she became his wife. When they came together, the LORD made her conceive, and she bore a son. Then the women said to Naomi, "Blessed be the LORD, who has not left you this day without next-of-kin; and may his name be renowned in Israel! He shall be to you a restorer of life and a nourisher of your old age; for your daughter-in-law who loves you, who is more to you than seven sons, has borne him." Then Naomi took the child and laid him in her bosom, and became his nurse. The women of the neighborhood gave him a name, saying, "A son has been born to Naomi." They named him Obed; he became the father of Jesse, the father of David.

They tell me that the most thoroughly read section of a daily newspaper is the Letters to the Editor. Not the sports page, nor the comics, nor the national columnists, but the letters to the editor. Now I have to confess that I sometimes skip this section entirely, and I usually give it only a quick glance, to see if there's a letter from someone I know. But several years ago I stumbled upon a letter that captured my interest. The writer (a person unknown to me) was registering her objection to a proposed law. To make her point she said, "A child conceived illegitimately is not in God's plan for procreation."

I understood what she was saying, and I agreed with her basic contention. I wish, as much as she did, that no children were conceived out of wedlock. In the purest, absolute sense, what the woman said is true. Such conceptions are not in God's plan. If everything in our world happened according to God's plan, I think each person would be born into a home where the parents were married and where the child would be loved—and where it would be reared with enough food to eat, proper medical care, and a chance for a good education. And also, with parents who would never make a mistake in rearing the child. But everything in our world isn't working the way God planned it.

But I'm happy to tell you that God is better than his plans. And while I wish everything in our world had gone according to God's plans, I must say that I am in awe of God, not so much for his wondrous plans as for the fact that he is better than those plans.

I'm thinking just now of a Jewish man named Elimelech and his wife, Naomi. They lived in bad times, in the period that is known in the Bible as the time of the judges, a period of particularly unstable government. To make it worse, nature conspired against them and famine swept the land. So Elimelech and Naomi did what would otherwise have been for them unthinkable; they moved to Moab.

It's always difficult for someone to migrate from one country to another. It means learning a whole new set of customs and feeling like an outsider—often an unwelcome outsider. But more was involved in this instance, a great deal more. For generations there had been enmity between the Israelites and the Moabites, an enmity which ran so deep that the Israelites were commanded, in the book of Deuteronomy, that they should not allow a Moabite to enter the assembly of their people; not even to the tenth generation (Deuteronomy 23:3). In truth, "tenth generation" was probably just a poetic way of saying *forever.* The Moabites were outsiders, and were meant to remain that way. Perhaps it was the only way the Israelites could maintain their ethnic purity. In any event, if you accept the thinking of the book of Deuteronomy, you have to conclude that this was God's plan.

Elimelech and Naomi were in such hard times that obedience to such a law was a luxury they couldn't afford, so with their two sons they moved to Moab. It must have been a terribly painful decision. Sometime thereafter, Elimelech died. I wonder if some of their old friends back home said, when they heard the news, "It's too bad, but you could have expected it. They did the wrong thing when they moved to Moab. They were just asking for trouble."

Even worse, the two young sons fell in love with Moabite girls and married them. Imagine, then, how the scandalmongers talked back home! Still more time passed by and the two young men died, leaving three widows, two of them quite young and the other in her middle or later years. It could hardly have been a more dismal picture, because in that time and place a woman without a husband, a father, or a brother couldn't hope to survive, unless perhaps it would be by prostitution.

You may well know the rest of the story. Naomi decided to return to her homeland, Israel, where she could hope to locate some distant relative who would be responsible for her. One daughter-in-law, Ruth, chose to go with her. It was a brave, loving, illogical decision, considering how unwelcome she would be. But in Israel she caught the eye and soon the affections of a well-to-do older man named Boaz. They married and had a child. That child became the grandfather of David, the greatest and most revered of Israel's kings.

Now it would surely seem that this wasn't according to the plans. A Moabite wasn't supposed to be accepted in Israel, not even to the tenth generation. Yet it turns out that this Moabite woman, Ruth, becomes the great-grandmother of the king Israel honored the most. And that's not all. When you get to the New Testament and read Matthew's list of Jesus' ancestry, you find that Ruth was an ancestress of the Messiah, Jesus our Lord.

All of which is to say that God is better than his plans.

Consider another Old Testament story. When this same David was king of Israel, he became enamored with a beautiful woman who was, unfortunately, married. She was, in fact, the wife of one of David's premier army officers. David committed adultery with her; then, to cover his crime, he arranged for the death of her husband so he could marry her. Believe me, that isn't the way God plans things. And God's prophet, Nathan, told David as much in fierce and unmistakable terms. He said that the child who had been conceived in their illegitimate union would die, as it did.

This is an ugly story. It seems that no good, none whatsoever, could possibly come from it. But later David and Bathsheba had another son. This son was Solomon, who succeeded David as king of Israel and who is still referred to as the wisest man that ever lived.

I think that if you and I were running things, we might have written off the union of David and Bathsheba as a total loss. Their romance had been born in lust and illegitimacy and was nurtured in deceit and murder. None of this was the way God would plan it. But God redeemed the ugly situation, because God is always better than his plans.

The truth is, if God allowed himself to be fenced in by his plans, there wouldn't be much room for the development of our human story. As Madeleine L'Engle points out, the people of God aren't all good, moral people. Often they are people who do quite wicked things. Often the best thing that can be said for them, she continues, is that when they fail, they pick themselves up, with God's help, and try again.

But this means that there's a constant tension in the scriptures between quality and grace, or between expectation and performance. A tension, that is, between God's plan and what God does with what we human beings give him. The scriptures tell us to speak the truth, but Abraham and Sarah lied in order to save Abraham's life. Yet Abraham is described as "the friend of God." The Law said the people should love the Lord their God with all their heart, soul, mind, and strength (Deuteronomy 6:5), but the writer of 2 Chronicles says of King Amaziah that "he did what was pleasing to the LORD, but did it reluctantly" (2 Chronicles 25:2 GNB). The seventh commandment says, "You shall not commit adultery," but the son of an adulterous relationship, Jephthah, became one of God's chosen instruments as a judge of Israel (Judges 11).

And that's the way the biblical record goes, chapter after chapter, Old Testament and New. God has a plan, and has commandments, and has divine expectations, but human beings fall short. Does God say, then, "These human beings have destroyed my dreams, so hereafter I'll use angels?" Not at all, thanks be to God! God seems rather to say, ten million times over, "Let's see what can be done with the confusion these human beings have given me." God's laws are strict, but God's character is gracious. God is better than his plans.

Does this give license for misconduct? Some people in the first century apparently thought so. They reasoned that if God's grace was demonstrated in mercy toward their sins, then the more they sinned, the more the grace of God would be seen (Romans 6:15ff.). But I think most of us would offer a different testimony. We have found that the more surely we have experienced the grace of God, the more surely we want to live worthy of its glory and beauty.

Watch God, the artist, at work, and be astonished. I see an artist with a fresh canvas, a supply of oils. He produces a masterpiece, and I view it with awe. Now I see another canvas. A fumbling novice has been struggling with it, and despite his good and earnest intentions, he has made a mess of things. You might almost think his aim was confusion. As he looks in despair at what he has done, he wants to throw it all away; nothing can redeem such a sorry affair as this.

Instead, he asks the Master Artist to see if there's any hope at all for this chaotic combination of colors. Slowly, steadily, surely the Master works, until at last he produces a canvas of surprising beauty. I don't really think it is what he would have made of this canvas if he had been able to work it from the beginning, but I marvel that he has brought so much beauty out of what was once nothing but disaster and confusion.

I am more impressed by the skill of the Artist in the second instance than in the first. And of course that's what I mean when I say that God is better than his plans. He shows how wondrous a Master he is, not by what he does with a perfect page—something we seem never to give him!—but by the skill with which he takes our confusions and turns them into an astonishing measure of order and beauty.

The late William Barclay visited one day with a psychiatrist in a leading British mental hospital. Barclay expressed his envy of the psychiatrist, because he could so often see the results of his work. But the psychiatrist answered, "Let me tell you something. All that a psychiatrist can do is to strip a person naked until you get down to the essential person; and if the essential person is bad stuff, there is nothing he can do about it." Turning to Barclay as a cleric, he continued, "That's where you come in."

In recalling the conversation, Barclay said, "I think he meant, that is where *Jesus Christ* comes in" (William Barclay, *In the Hands of God*, 118).

And that's the point of all I'm saying. That's what Christian salvation is about, and that's something of what we mean by the grace of God.

There are times in life when a voice will tell you that you've ruined everything. Sometimes the voice will come from some human being, even a well-meaning one, and sometimes it will simply rise up within your own soul—and those are the times when the voice is most persuasive! The voice will sound logical, because from what you can see, you have for sure ruined things. And whatever the judgment the voice passes on you, it will seem fair enough, because when a person messes things up, he or she should expect to pay the penalty. The voice will also seem moral, like the words in the letter to the editor to which I referred earlier.

But however logical, just, and moral the voice may seem, I insist that it is the voice of the devil, because it is a voice which not only denies the grace of God, but which also seeks to keep us from recognizing that such grace exists. Even if such a statement is well-intended, it fails to reckon with the power of the Master Artist of the universe.

Because God is ready always, at our invitation, to take the canvas of our lives, corrupted both by our mistakes and also by the mistakes and sometimes the unkindness and cruelty of others, and to begin reworking the canvas.

What God gets in the end will not be what was originally planned, because the original plan, it seems to me, was for a Garden of Eden, a place of perfection. But it will be a wondrous sight, a redeemed life. And all through eternity you will want to sing a song of grace: God is better than his plans.

Suggestions for Leading a Study of
Old Testament Stories from the Back Side

Old Testament Stories from the Back Side is a collection of twelve essays designed to stimulate our thinking about our faith, our relationships with others, and how God is at work in our world today. This leader's guide is intended to assist you in facilitating a discussion group, so that the experience is beneficial for both you and your group.

As a discussion leader, you have the opportunity to help others obtain the answers they are seeking on their spiritual journey. The conversations in your group may cover a variety of topics as together you ask questions and seek answers. Here are some thoughts on how you can help your group:

1. Distribute the book to participants before your first group meeting and request that they come having read the first chapter. You may want to limit the size of your group to increase participation.

2. Participants may ask what the title of this book means. The "back side" means simply a different perspective in order to gain new insights about ourselves, others, and our faith.

3. Begin your session on time. Your participants will appreciate meetings that begin when scheduled and end when promised. You may want to begin your first session with introductions and a brief get-acquainted time. Start each session by reading aloud the snap-shot summary of the chapter for the day.

4. Select discussion questions and activities in advance. Note that the first question is usually a general question designed to get the discussion going. Feel free to change the order of the listed questions and create your own questions. Allow a set amount of time for the questions and activities.

5. Remind your participants that all questions are valid as part of the learning process. Encourage their participation in discussion by saying that there are no "wrong" answers and that all input will be appreciated. Invite them to share their thoughts, personal stories, and ideas as their comfort level dictates.

6. Some questions may be more difficult to answer than others. If you ask a question and no one responds, begin the discussion by venturing an answer yourself. Then ask for comments and other answers. Remember that some questions may have multiple answers.

7. Ask the question "Why?" or "Why do you believe that?" to help continue a discussion and give it greater depth.

8. Give everyone a chance to talk. Keep the conversation moving. Occasionally you may want to direct a question at a specific person who has been quiet. "Do you have anything to add?" is a good follow-up question to another person. If the topic of conversation gets off track, move ahead by asking the next question in your leader's guide.

9. Before moving from questions to activities, ask members if they have any questions that have not been answered. Remember that as a leader, you do not have to know all the answers. Some answers may come from group members. Other answers may even need a bit of research. Your job is to keep the discussion moving and to encourage participation.

10. Review the activity in advance. Feel free to modify it or create your own activity. Encourage participants to try the home activity. You might want to discuss the home activity at a future meeting.

11. Following the conclusion of the activity, close with a brief prayer; either the printed prayer in the leader's guide or one of your own. If your group desires, pause for individual prayer petitions.

12. Be grateful and supportive. Thank members for their ideas and participation.

13. You are not expected to be a "perfect" leader. Just do the best you can by focusing on the participants and the lesson. God will help you lead this group.

14. Enjoy your time together.

CHAPTER 1

The Second Sin

Snapshot Summary

This book looks at twelve Old Testament stories from the "back side." The "back side" means simply a different or fresh perspective in order to gain new insights about our faith. This first chapter looks at how excuses and our unwillingness to admit sin can separate us from God.

Discussion Questions

1. What insights did you receive from this chapter?
2. Why does one sin often lead to a second one?
3. How is the Second Sin related to the Unpardonable Sin?
4. What are common reasons we sometimes refuse to confess or repent?
5. What is your response when someone admits a mistake to you?
6. Describe a time when you had to admit doing something wrong.
7. Why are excuses so dangerous?
8. When are excuses justified?
9. What would God have us do rather than offer an excuse?
10. How do excuses separate us from other people?

Activities

As a group: Write a list of excuses for being angry with someone. Examine each excuse one by one and determine if the excuse has any validity. What can be learned from examining our excuses?

At home: Make an effort to avoid making excuses to others during the coming week. Try to admit mistakes and apologize for errors. See how people respond.

Prayer: Forgiving Father, help us to be honest with you and others when we make mistakes. Thank you for your love and grace which knows no bounds. Amen.

The Importance of Naming Joseph

Snapshot Summary

Chapter 1 showed us the importance of honesty in our relationships with God and all people. This chapter helps us understand the purpose and goodness of God through the eyes of Rachel.

Discussion Questions

1. What insights did you receive from this chapter?
2. How did your parents arrive at your name? Is there any special meaning?
3. Why do we often ask God for "more"? Why do we hesitate to do so sometimes?
4. Describe a time when you should have asked God for more but didn't.
5. How can one blessing build upon another?
6. What causes us to think small and expect little?
7. Name an important blessing that came unexpectedly in your life after a long time.
8. What made Rachel a remarkable woman?
9. For what reasons does God bless us and give us abundance?
10. Why does God have us wait for blessings sometimes?

Activities

As a group: Each person writes down twenty ways he or she has been blessed by God and then exchanges sheets with another person in the group. Each person then shares with the group how his or her "partner" has been blessed.

At home: Start a Blessings Bank by making a container that holds slips of paper that recall things you are thankful for. Try to make a bank deposit each day and include a coin with each deposit. Read the slips at the end of each week, or save them to read on Thanksgiving Day. Give the coins to charity each year.

Prayer: *Jesus, we thank you for our many blessings and for your goodness in continuing to give us more. Help us to be as generous with others, especially those who are not as fortunate as we are. Amen.*

Because My Mother Told Me

Snapshot Summary

Chapter 2 showed us how we thank God best by accepting his divine kindness and asking for more of the same as Rachel did. Chapter 3 shows how we "catch" things from others and influence people by our witness.

Discussion Questions

1. What insights did you receive from this chapter?
2. Name one big lesson you learned early in life. Who taught it to you?
3. Share something important that you have learned outside a classroom. How has this learning influenced or changed your life?
4. Name an influential person in your life. Briefly share how this person has helped you.
5. In what ways do we influence others? As far as you are aware, how have you influenced others in your life?
6. How can you tell a good influence from a bad influence?
7. What did you find interesting about the story of Moses?
8. How does our relationship with God influence our lives?
9. What makes people influential? Name some nationally influential people.
10. Who or what influenced you to become a Christian?

Activities

As a group: Pair up with a partner and role play that one of you is in jail and the other has the key to your cell and can set you free. Take turns being in jail and trying to influence the jailer. Spend about three minutes each. Report your results to the group. Share any insights about influencing others that you gained from this activity.

At home: Write a thank you letter to someone who has influenced you.

> **Prayer:** God, we thank you for those who have influenced us in our spiritual journey. Bless them as they have blessed us. Help each of us to be a good influence to others. Amen.

Moses' Mid-Life Crisis

Snapshot Summary

The last chapter helped us remember that others influence us and that we influence others through our words and deeds. Chapter 4 shows us how a crisis can be an opportunity for God to accomplish great things.

Discussion Questions

1. What insights did you receive from this chapter?
2. What was your most difficult birthday and why?
3. When do you think middle-age begins and why?
4. What images come to mind when you hear the words "mid-life crisis"?
5. What was unique about Moses' mid-life crisis?
6. What dream have you let go of as you have grown older? Why?
7. Do you think people can avoid having a mid-life crisis? How?
8. What are signs that a crisis—any crisis—has started? That one has ended?
9. What has been the cause of a crisis in your life?
10. What would God have us do with each crisis we face?

Activities

As a group: Have one person in the group fabricate a crisis. After listening to the story, offer solutions, insights, and help to the individual. After ten to fifteen minutes, the person in crisis should respond to the group.

At home: Locate and read a magazine article on how to cope with a crisis or how to help people in crisis.

Prayer: *Dear God, we thank you that you are always with us and that you can turn any crisis into something good. Help us to remember your love for us. Amen.*

Patron Saint of the Minority Report

Snapshot Summary

Chapter 4 showed us how God can use a crisis to accomplish good in our life and the lives of others. Chapter 5 tells the story of Caleb and how God can use a minority to influence the majority.

Discussion Questions

1. What insights did you receive from this chapter?
2. What caused Caleb to voice his minority opinion? Why didn't he just keep quiet?
3. What did you find most interesting about Caleb's story?
4. When have you been in the minority? How did it feel?
5. Based on your own experience, what are the good and bad aspects of committees? How has a committee you have served on supported or suppressed a minority opinion?
6. Give an example of something you wanted to do in response to a minority view you held but were afraid to do.
7. Why does it take faith to hold a minority view?
8. Give examples of how God sometimes sides with the minority.
9. What minorities exist within a church?
10. How should the church treat those minority groups?

Activities

As a group: Write down as many minorities as you can think of that exist in the United States. Discuss how they have influenced our culture.

At home: Select one of the minorities that you know least about and read a magazine article about this group.

Prayer: *Dear Lord, we praise you that you have made us to be individuals, different from one another. Help us to remember that we all were created by you and belong to you. Amen.*

CHAPTER 6

Tragic Son, Tragic Father

Snapshot Summary

The last chapter focused on minorities and how God can use them to achieve his purposes. Chapter 6 helps us better understand God's grace in relationship to tragedy.

Discussion Questions

1. What insights did you receive from this chapter?
2. Why is this story a classic tragedy?
3. Why is it so easy for tragedy to lead to more tragedy?
4. When you were growing up, did you know someone who was "different" from the others? How was that person treated?
5. Have you ever felt "different" from others? How?
6. Have you ever been trapped by a commitment? Explain.
7. How can we as Christians avoid the mistake that Jephthah made?
8. How do you feel about Jephthah the person?
9. What did Jephthah not know about God's grace?
10. Have you ever worked hard for something, only to lose something else in the process? Explain. How was God's grace a part of your experience?

Activities

As a group: Role play a situation in which one person is Jephthah and the rest of the group are Christians who, in light of God's grace, are trying to talk him out of sacrificing his daughter. Both should defend their positions.

At home: Share the story of Jephthah with someone and what it means to you.

Prayer: *Dear God, your grace is amazing, and we thank you for your goodness to us. Help us to remember that you are with us in all our difficult situations. Amen.*

CHAPTER 7

Honey in the Lion

Snapshot Summary

Chapter 6 showed how we sometimes can lose what means the most to us, as Jephthah did. This chapter helps us understand how we can face adversity and life's troubles knowing that God can bring good out of any situation.

Discussion Questions

1. What insights did you receive from this chapter?
2. Recall a riddle you once heard or created.
3. After reading this chapter, what does the phrase "honey in the lion" mean to you?
4. Describe a time when you faced a "lion."
5. Have you ever found "honey in a lion"? Explain.
6. Have you ever lost a battle to a "lion"?
7. How does faith and God help you conquer adversity?
8. Are Christians better at finding "honey" than non-Christians?
9. What key actions do we need to take to find "honey in the lion"?
10. What dangers are there in reaching for the "honey"?

Activities

As a group: Choose an event or situation that was a "lion" on a national or international scale, such as World War II, and brainstorm some of the good that came about during and after the event.

At home: Write a list of the "lions" you have faced in your life. Reflect on how God played a role in each situation.

Prayer: Jesus, we thank you for the "lions" we face in life and how they strengthen us to be of better service to you. Help us to be aware of the goodness that is all around us. Amen.

Beauty and the Beast

Snapshot Summary

Chapter 7 helped us see how God can bring good things from adversity. Chapter 8 is the story of Abigail and Nabal and how we can live in a world of troubles and goodness.

Discussion Questions

1. What insights did you receive from this chapter?
2. What impressed you about the story of Abigail and Nabal?
3. Did you think Abigail did the right thing by going to David? What other choices did she have?
4. How do our relationships and our environment affect our lives and our accomplishments?
5. Name some modern-day beasts and beauties.
6. Have you ever encountered a beast that became a beauty? Explain.
7. What happens when life's beasts cannot be changed?
8. What is your favorite movie with a happy ending? Why?
9. What has helped you to live with the handicaps and troubles in your life?
10. How does God want us to deal with the beasts in our lives?

Activities

As a group: Go through a national magazine and classify the photos as either beauties or beasts. What makes some decisions difficult?

At home: Identify and pray for a "beast" or those who face them.

Prayer: *Dear God, thank you for the goodness and good people in this world. Help us to share your love with others, even those we don't understand. Amen.*

A Refugee at the King's Table

Snapshot Summary

Chapter 8 showed us the struggles of beauties who face the beasts of the world. This chapter tells us about God's grace and communion using the story of Mephibosheth.

Discussion Questions

1. What insights did you receive from this chapter?
2. Why is the story of Mephibosheth a story about grace?
3. What does it mean to be a refugee? Have you ever felt like a refugee?
4. What impressed you about the story of Mephibosheth?
5. What traits do we share with Mephibosheth?
6. What traits did you inherit from your parents?
7. In what ways are we (humans) victims of circumstance?
8. In what ways do people hide their helplessness and deformities?
9. What did you learn about communion from this chapter?
10. In what way is David's acceptance of Mephibosheth like God's acceptance of us?

Activities

As a group: Share Holy Communion together.
At home: Pray for the refugees of the world.

> **Prayer:** *Dear God, thank you for Holy Communion. We are grateful that we can always come to you and to your table. Help us to remember your love as we strive to love others. Amen.*

In Defense of Job's Wife

Snapshot Summary

In the last chapter we learned about acceptance and God's grace through the story of Mephibosheth. In this chapter we learn about what it means and costs to be supportive.

Discussion Questions

1. What insights did you receive from this chapter? What specific insights about Job and Job's wife did you receive?
2. Who had it worse: Job or Job's wife? Explain.
3. Do you agree with the author's assessment of Job's wife? What is your impression of her?
4. How has someone supported you or someone you know during a period of misfortune?
5. What are other ways of supporting someone during tough times?
6. Describe a time when you wanted to help someone who was suffering, but you didn't know how to do it. How did you feel?
7. What makes it hard to play a supporting role sometimes?
8. What "costs" have you experienced when being supportive of someone else?
9. How is giving support to someone who has experienced a major loss different from giving support to others in need?
10. How can you support someone who is being supportive of someone else?

Activities

As a group: Discuss the feelings of someone who has been victimized by crime. How could you offer support?

At home: Make note of newspaper stories about people who are suffering a loss. Pray for them this week.

> **Prayer:** *Jesus, you are always there to support us. Help us to be there for others and to offer your love to them. Amen.*

CHAPTER 11

Jonah's Christmas Story

Snapshot Summary

Chapter 10 explored issues related to support and sacrifices made for others. This chapter relates the story of Jonah to Christmas as an example of God's grace.

Discussion Questions

1. What insights did you receive from this chapter? What specific insights about Jonah did you receive? About Christmas?
2. Have you ever tried to run away from God? Explain.
3. Have you ever been "swallowed up by a fish"? Explain.
4. What do we learn about God's love from Jonah's story?
5. In what way is Jonah's story a Christmas story?
6. Why does the author say Christmas is the very essence of grace?
7. Why is it difficult at times to catch God's Christmas spirit?
8. What can we do to overcome these obstacles?
9. Describe a time when you felt unlovable like the city of Nineveh.
10. How did this chapter change your view of Christmas?

Activities

As a group: Share together your happiest Christmas memories.

At home: Write a list of gifts that God has given you during the Christmas season over the years. Share it with a family member.

Prayer: *Dear Lord, thank you for your grace, which comes to us during all seasons of the year but especially at Christmas. Open our eyes so that we may see your gifts more clearly. Amen.*

God Is Better Than His Plans

Snapshot Summary

Chapter 11 explored God's grace through the story of Jonah and the season of Christmas. Chapter 12 continues to show us new aspects of God's grace in light of our mistakes and failed plans.

Discussion Questions

1. What insights did you receive from this chapter?
2. How was God's grace evident in the lives of Naomi, Ruth, and David?
3. In what ways is God better than his plans? How has this proved true through the ages?
4. Describe a time when your plans went wrong.
5. How does it feel to start over again? Give examples from your own experience.
6. How is God like the Master Artist?
7. What has God done with some of your mistakes?
8. How should we respond to God's wonderful grace?
9. What opportunities do we have as Christians because God is better than his plans?
10. Who first taught you about God's grace? What was your first lesson about God's grace?

Activities

As a group: Brainstorm what the world would be like if everything went according to God's plan. Focus on career, family, and relationships. What would it be like to live in such a world?

At home: Make a list of mistakes you have made. Beside each, describe any good that has come from the mistake. Thank God for these blessings made possible through God's abundant grace.

Prayer: God, we praise you for your amazing grace. Thank you for giving us this time together to learn more about you and ourselves. Be with us as we go our separate ways and continue to encourage us with your love. Amen.